Anonymous

The Holy Bible Abridged

Or, The History of the Old and New Testament

Anonymous

The Holy Bible Abridged
Or, The History of the Old and New Testament

ISBN/EAN: 9783744749558

Printed in Europe, USA, Canada, Australia, Japan

Cover: Foto ©Lupo / pixelio.de

More available books at **www.hansebooks.com**

And the serpent said unto the woman, Ye shall not surely die.
GENESIS iii. 4.

THE HOLY BIBLE ABRIDGED:

OR, THE HISTORY

OF THE

Old and New Testament.

Illustrated with Notes, and adorned with Cuts,

For the Use of Childrens.

Suffer little children to *come unto me, and forbid them not.* Luke xviii. 16.

THE SECOND *WORCESTER* EDITION.

WORCESTER, (MASSACHUSETTS)
FROM THE PRESS OF
THOMAS, SON & THOMAS,
AND SOLD AT THEIR BOOKSTORE.
MDCCXCVI.

TO THE
PARENTS, GUARDIANS,
AND
GOVERNESSES
OF THE
UNITED STATES,
THIS
HISTORY
OF THE
OLD AND NEW TESTAMENTS

Is humbly inscribed,

By their obedient,

Humble Servants,

The PUBLISHERS.

PREFACE.

THE author's design in this publication is evidently to give children such a taste of the writings of the Holy penman, as may engage them earnestly and seriously in the study of the sacred books of the Old and New Testaments.

To forward them in this laudable and pious pursuit, he has selected such portions of the Scriptures as are both instructive and entertaining; such as will not only

PREFACE.

only feed the fancy, but mend the heart, and eſtabliſh in the mind thoſe unalterable laws of the DEITY, which lead us to the knowledge of himſelf, which cement us together in ſociety, and on which our happineſs both in this life and the next muſt abſolutely depend.

To render this little book the more pleaſing to children, it is embelliſhed with a great number of cuts; and, that it may be uſeful to thoſe more advanced in years, the chronology of the moſt remarkable Events is preſerved, and ſuch notes interſperſed as he had reaſon to apprehend would be uſeful.

This

PREFACE.

This is the author's design, which, he is persuaded, every good Christian will approve; and he hopes that he has been careful to execute it in such a manner, as to spare himself the pains of an apology to the Publick.

THE CONTENTS,

PART I.

The OLD TESTAMENT.

	Page.
CHAP. I. TREATING of GOD.	17
CHAP. II. Of the CREATION.	18
CHAP. III. Of the Garden of EDEN.	26
CHAP. IV. Of ADAM and EVE in Paradise, their fall and expulsion.	29
CHAP. V. The Consequences of the FALL.	32

CHAP.

CONTENTS.

Chap. VI.
Of the Flood. — Page 34

Chap. VII.
The World divided amongst Noah's three Sons, and the Building of the Tower of Babel. — 37

Chap. VIII.
The Birth and Call of Abraham, and the Promise made to him—Sodom and Gomorrah destroyed; Isaac born. — 39

Chap. IX.
Of Joseph and his Brethren. — 43

Chap. X.
The Oppression of the Children of Israel in Egypt, and their Deliverance from thence. — 55

Chap. XI.
Pharaoh and his Host drowned in the

CONTENTS.

                                    Page.
the Red Sea,—The *Murmurings
of the* Israelites.   61

Chap. XII.
The Law *published on Mount* Sinai. — 64

Chap. XIII.
Of the Brazen Serpent.—*The Story
of* BALAAM *and his* Ass. —   69

Chap. XIV.
The Israelites *pass through* Jordan, *and take* Jericho—*The Sun and Moon stand still—The History of* SAMSON—SAUL *anointed King—The Story of* DAVID *and* GOLIAH—*The Reign of* DAVID. — 74

Chap. XV.
SOLOMON's *Wisdom. His Judgment between the two Harlots. The Building and Dedication of the Temple. History of the Prophets* ELIJAH *and* ELISHA. JEZEBEL *eaten by Dogs.* — —   91

                              CHAP.

CHAP. XVI.

Jonah in the Whale's Belly— Shadrach, Meshach, and Abednego cast into a fiery Furnace— Daniel in the Lion's Den— The Jewish history brought down to the Birth of Christ. ——— 104

PART II.

THE NEW TESTAMENT.

CHAP. I. Page.

THE Birth of CHRIST—The Angel appears to the Shepherds—The Adoration of the MAGI—CHRIST disputes with the Doctors in the Temple. — — — — — — 117

CHAP. II.

CHRIST baptized by JOHN—Enters upon his Ministry—His Sermon on the Mount. — — — — 125

CHAP. III.

CHRIST restores the Widow's Son to Life—He stilleth the Tempest—
JOHN

CONTENTS.

Page.

JOHN *the Baptist beheaded—Five Thousand fed with five loaves and two Fishes*—CHRIST *walks on the Sea and St.* PETER *comes to meet him.* ——— ——— ——— 133

CHAP. IV.

*The Good Samaritan—The Prodigal Son—*Dives *and* Lazarus. — 140

CHAP. V.

Lazarus *raised from the Dead—*CHRIST *rides to* Jerusalem *on an Ass—The Institution of the Lord's Supper—*CHRIST *betrayed by* Judas, *carried before* Caiaphas, *and denied by* Peter. ——— 147

CHAP. VI.

The Crucifixion, Resurrection and Ascension of CHRIST. ——— ——— 153

CHAP. VII.

The Descent of the HOLY GHOST— Annanias

CONTENTS.

Page.

Annanias *and* Sapphira *struck dead for telling a Lie*—St. Stephen *stoned.* — — — — 159

CHAP. VIII.

The miraculous Conversion of St. Paul —St. Peter *delivered out of prison by an Angel*—St. Paul *shipwrecked.* —— —— 164

CONCLUSION.

Of the LAST JUDGMENT. —— 171

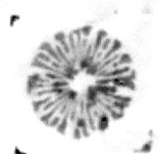

THE HISTORY OF THE HOLY BIBLE.

Chap. I.

Treating of GOD.

GOD is in himself from eternity to eternity, without beginning and without end, the most perfect and blessed Being: In his substance, spiritual and eternal; In his person, three, united in one; in his name, Father, Son, and Holy Ghost; in his will, holy, just, merciful and true; in power, omnipotent; in wisdom, incomprehensible; a light unto which none can approach, yet all in all; omnipresent in every place; the highest good,

good, and the only inexhaustible fountain of all goodness; the Creator of all things, and the director, Protector, Preserver, and Sustainer of them all.

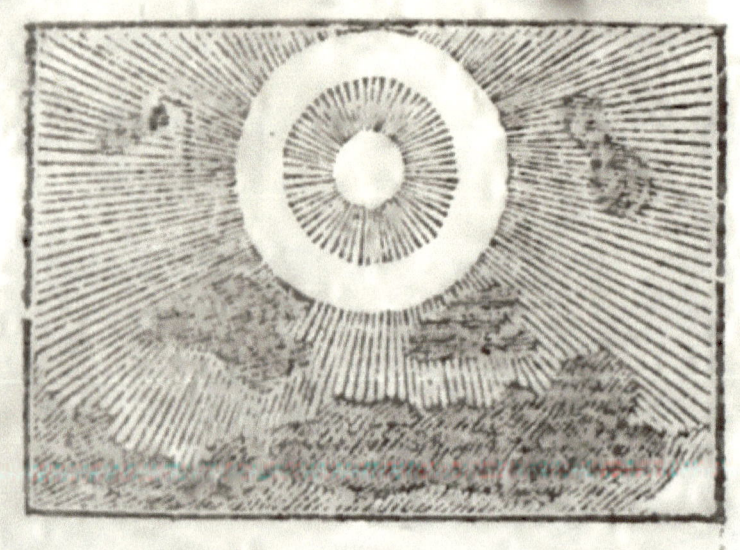

Chap. II.

Of the Creation.

IN the beginning God created the heaven and the earth. And the earth was without form and void, and darkness was upon the face of the deep; and the spirit of God moved upon the face of the waters. And God said, Let there be light;

THE HOLY BIBLE.

light; and there was light. And God saw the light, that it was good; and God divided the light from the darkneſs. And God called the light *Day*, and the darkneſs he called *Night*: And the evening and the morning were the firſt day.

And God ſaid, Let there be a firmament in the midſt of the waters, and let it divide the water from the waters. And God made the firmament, and divided the waters which were under the firmament from the waters which were above the firmament: And it was ſo. And God called the firmament *Heaven*: And the

the evening and the morning were the second day.

And God said, Let the waters under the heaven be gathered together unto one place, and let the dry land appear; and it was so. And God called the dry land *Earth*, and the gathering together of the waters called he *Seas*: And God saw that it was good. And God said, Let the earth bring forth grass, the herb yielding seed, and the fruit tree yielding fruit after his kind, whose seed is in itself upon the earth: And it was so. And

And the earth brought forth grafs, and herb yielding feed after his kind, and the tree yielding fruit, whofe feed was in itfelf, after his kind: And God faw that it was good. And the evening and the morning, were the third day.

And God faid, Let there be lights in the firmament of the heaven to divide the day from the night: And let them be for figns, and feafons, and for days and years. And let them be for lights in the firmament of the heaven, to give light upon the earth: And it was fo. And God made two great lights; the
greater

greater light to rule the day, and the lesser light to rule the night; he made the stars also. And God set them in the firmament of the heaven to give light upon the earth, and to rule over the day and over the night, and to divide the light from the darkness: And God saw that it was good. And the evening and the morning were the fourth day.*

*The inspired author of this account of the creation hath told us before, under the first day's creation, *Gen.* i. 3. *that God said, 'Let there be light, and there was light*, whence we may reasonably conclude, that the sun, moon, and stars were then created, though the chaos might not be sufficiently separated and disposed to render them distinct; and if so, this portion of scripture can only mean that the air being perfectly freed from those thick vapours that had from the first day obscured these glorious *luminaries*, they on the fourth day appeared to the earth in all their splendour and magnificence.

And

THE HOLY BIBLE. 23

And God said, let the waters bring forth abundantly the moving creature that hath life, and fowl that may fly above the earth in the open firmament of heaven. And God created great whales, and every living creature that moveth, which the waters brought forth abundantly after their kind : And God saw that it was good. And God bleſſed them, ſaying, Be fruitful, and multiply, and fill the waters in the ſeas, and let fowls multiply in the earth. And the evening and the morning were the fifth day.
And

And God said, Let the earth bring forth the living creature after his kind, cattle and creeping thing, and beast of the earth after his kind; and it was so. And God made the beast of the earth after his kind, and cattle after their kind, and every thing that creepeth upon the earth after his kind: And God saw that it was good, and God said, Let us make man in our image, after our likeness; and let him have dominion over the fish of the sea, and over the fowl of the air, and over cattle, and over all the earth, and over every creeping thing that creepeth upon the earth. So

So God created man in his own image, in the image of God created he him; male and female created he them. And God blessed them, and God said unto them, Be fruitful and multiply, and replenish the earth, and subdue it, and have dominion over the fish of the sea, and over the fowl of the air, and over every living thing that creepeth upon the earth. And God said, Behold I have given you every herb bearing seed, which is upon the face of all the earth, and every tree, in the which is the fruit of a tree yielding seed; to you it shall be for meat. And to every beast of the earth, and to the fowl of the air, and to every thing that creepeth upon the earth, wherein there is life, I have given every green herb for meat; and it was so. And God saw every thing that he had made, and behold it was very good. And the evening and the morning were the sixth day.*

CHAP.

*Though *Moses* makes no mention of the Angelick Hosts, in his account of the creation, yet the expositors of the scriptures are of opinion that the other places in holy writ sufficient-

Chap. III.

Of the Garden of EDEN.

THUS the heavens and the earth were finished, and all the host of them. And on the seventh day God ended his work which he had made; and God blessed the seventh day, and sanctified it, because that in it he had rested* from all his work, the creation of all things being finished, and the work entirely made. And the Lord God formed man *(that he made)* of the dust of the ground and breathed into his nostrils the breath of life;

ly intimate that those myriads of Angels which stand before the throne of God, were on the first day created with the light. And these God hath formed spiritual, amicable Beings, whose natures we cannot comprehend.

*The *resting* of God being spoken after the manner of men, implieth not any weariness in him, for *the Creator of the ends of the earth fainteth not, neither is he weary*. Isa. xi. 28. Is was by the ancients made a symbol of the rest of the just from all their labours; when all grief, sorrow, and sighing shall fly away, and God shall be all in all.

life; and man became a living soul. And the Lord God planted a Garden eastward in *Eden*; and there he put the man whom he had formed. And out of the ground made the Lord God to grow every tree that is pleasant to the sight and good for food; the tree of life also in the midst of the garden, and the tree of knowledge of good and evil. And a river went out of *Eden* to water the garden; and from thence it was parted, and became into four heads. The name of the first is *Pison*: That is it which compasseth the whole land of *Havilah*, where there is gold. And the name of the second river is *Gihon*: The same is it that compasseth the whole land of *Ethiopia*. And the name of the third river is *Hiddekel*: That is it which goeth towards the east of *Assyria*. And the fourth river is *Euphrates*. And the Lord God took the man and put him into the garden of *Eden*, to dress it and to keep it. And the Lord God commanded the man, saying, Of every tree of the garden thou mayest freely eat; but of the tree of knowledge

of

of good and evil, thou shalt not eat of it: For in the day that thou eatest thereof, thou shalt surely die. And the Lord God said, It is not good that the man should be alone; I will make him an helpmeet for him. And out of the ground the Lord God formed every beast of the field, and every fowl of the air, and brought them to *Adam*, to see what he would call them: And whatsoever *Adam* called every living creature, that was the name thereof. And *Adam* gave names to all cattle, and to the fowl of the air, and to every beast of the field; but for *Adam* there was not found an helpmeet for him. And the Lord God caused a deep sleep to fall upon *Adam*; and he took one of his ribs, and closed up the flesh instead thereof. And the rib which the Lord God had taken from man, made he a woman, and brought he unto the man. And *Adam* said, This is now bone of my bone, and flesh of my flesh; she shall be called *Woman*, because she was taken out of man.

CHAP.

THE HOLY BIBLE. 79

CHAP. IV.

Of ADAM *and* EVE *in Paradise, their Fall and Expulsion.*

OUR first parents thus planted in the garden of *Eden*, or terrestrial paradise, were perfectly happy, as they were perfectly innocent. Whilst they continued obedient to the divine command, their bliss was uninterrupted, all nature smiled around them; and, as they knew no sin, though *they were both naked they were not ashamed*. But they did not
long

long enjoy the comforts of this delightful situation; for the subtile serpent, (the Devil) by his artful insinuations, prevailed on the woman to eat of the forbidden fruit, which having tasted, she gave unto her husband. And he did eat also. By this transgression of the law of God, they lost their innocence and happiness together: Their eyes were opened; they became sensible of their nakedness; and conscious of their guilt, endeavoured to hide themselves from the presence of their offended creator amongst the trees of the garden. But this was a vain attempt, and equally vain were their excuses; the man laying the blame on the woman, and the woman on the serpent. Hereupon the Lord pronounced a heavy curse upon the serpent, by whose wiles sin and death were thus introduced into the world; but in the midst of his anger, taking pity on fallen man, he immediately promised that *the seed of the woman should bruise the Serpent's head*; by which is understood, that mankind should be delivered from sin, from death

and

and the power of the devil, by JESUS CHRIST, who should be born of a virgin. For *Eve*'s disobedience, God passed this sentence upon her, *I will multiply thy sorrow and thy conception; in sorrow shalt thou bring forth children and thy desire shall be to thy husband, and he shall rule over thee.* And unto *Adam* he said, *Cursed is the ground for thy sake; in sorrow shalt thou eat of it all the days of thy life. Thorns also and thistles shall it bring forth to thee; and thou shalt eat the herb of the field. In the sweat of thy face shalt thou eat bread, until thou returnest unto the ground; for out of it wast thou taken, for dust thou art, and unto dust thou shalt return.* Then were the fallen pair driven from their seat of bliss, and exposed to hardships, sorrow, sickness, and death itself; which are likewise the just lot of all their sinful posterity.

CHAP.

32 THE HISTORY OF

Chap. V.

The Consequence of the Fall.

THE seed of sin being sown in our first parents, soon showed its fatal effects in their immediate offspring, and afterwards in their most remote descendants; for Satan, having but too well succeeded in his first attempts upon the innocence of man, unweariedly pursued the advantages he had gained, in order to involve the whole human race in misery and destruction. A melancholy instance

stance of this we have in the story of *Cain* and *Abel*, the sons of *Adam* and *Eve*. The former who was a husbandman, *brought of the fruit of the ground an offering unto the Lord* ; and *Abel* who was a shepherd, *brought also of the firstlings of his flock, and of the fat thereof*. But *Cain* (whose heart was full of hatred and envy) finding his offering not so acceptable to God as that of *Abel*, was *very wrath*, and meditated revenge on his innocent brother. Accordingly when they were together in the field, he took the opportunity and *rose up against him and slew him*; but the blood of the righteous *Abel* cryed from the ground for vengence, God condemned *Cain* to be a *fugative and a vagabond in the earth*; setting a mark upon him that none might slay him, so that he might live to bear the stings of a wounded conscience.

However, though sin began to reign in the world so early, God was known to and worshipped by the Patriarchs, especially by the family of *Seth*, one of the sons of *Adam*. And amongst these Patriarchs

triarchs the Scripture mentions *Enoch*; who *walked with God, and God took him out of the World, so that he died not*; thereby remarkably rewarding his eminent piety and goodness, and pointing out to mankind a state of futurity. But in process of time the posterity of *Seth* was corrupted likewise and mingled with the wicked; insomuch that the *world was filled with violence*, and the corruption was so great and general, that God determined to destroyed the whole race of man by the flood, except righteous *Noah* and his family. To this purpose God commanded *Noah* to build an ark, in which he and his wife, his three sons, (*Shem, Ham*, and *Japheth*) and their wives, and the male and female of every species of fowl, cattle, and creeping things, should be preserved from the universal deluge.

CHAP. VI.
Of the FLOOD.

IT was in the year of the world 1656, before *Christ* 2346 and the 600th of *Noah's*

THE HOLY BIBLE. 35

Noah's age, that he and his family, and the several kinds of animals, as God had commanded, entered into the ark, which

had been an hundred years in building. This being done, *the fountains of the great deep were broken up, the windows of heaven were opened*, and such violent rains poured down for forty days and for forty nights, that the waters arose fifteen cubits above the highest mountains, and both man, cattle, creeping things *and the fowls of the heaven were destroyed, and* Noah *only remained alive, and they that were with him in the ark.* When the waters were confiderably abated, the
ark

ark rested on the mountains of *Ararat*; and having continued there several months, *Noah* sent forth a raven, which went to and fro; and after that a dove, which finding no resting place, came back to the ark, and he took her in. Seven days afterwards he sent out the dove, which returned with an olive leaf in her mouth: And having waited seven days longer he sent forth the same dove, but she returned no more; by which he knew that the waters were dried from off the earth. God then commanded *Noah* to come out of the ark, with his family and the living creatures, in which they had been shut up, according to our account of time, from the 29th of *October* to the 8th of *November* the following year, that is, one year and ten days.—— Man's life is now shortened.

Chap. VII.

The world divided amongst Noah's *three sons and the building of the* Tower of Babel.

NOAH began the new world by building an altar to the Lord; and he *took of every clean beast, and every clean fowl, and offered burnt offerings on the alter.* The Almighty accepted his sacrifice, graciously promising that *while the Earth remaineth, seed time and harvest, and cold and heat, and summer and winter, and day and night, shall not cease.* And God *set his bow in the clouds,* (the rainbow) in token of an everlasting covenant he made with *Noah* and all his posterity, that, he would never more destroy the world by a deluge.

Sixty seven years after the flood, *Heber*, a descendant of *Shem*, was born; from him came the *Hebrews* and the *Hebrew* language. About this time *Hebron*, afterwards the metropolis of *Judah*, was built. A hundred years after the flood,

Noah

Noah divided the earth among his three sons; *Judah* had the west of *Asia*, from the mountains *Taurus* and *Anan*, and all *Europe*. *Ham* had all *Arabia*, and all *Africa*. *Shem* had all the eastern *Asia*. Fourteen years after the earth was partitioned out among the sons of *Noah*, *Nimrod*, the grandson of *Ham*, laid the foundation of the *Babylonish* or *Assyrian*

Monarchy. And the world being now pretty well replenished with inhabitants they began to build the city and tower of *Babel*, vainly attempting to raise its walls to the very skies, in hopes of rendering their names immortal. But God soon baffled their impious project, by confounding their language so that they could not understand each other: And thence the tower was called *Babel*, which signifies confusion. The one language of the world was now divided into seventy two sorts (the *Hebrew* remaining in the posterity of *Heber*) and the distractions arising from hence not only put a stop to the building, but occasioned their dispersion over the face of the earth.——The city of *Babylon*, in some time, under another prince, became the metropolis of *Chaldea*. And soon after *Nineveh*, the metropolis of *Syria*, was built.

CHAP. VIII.

The Birth and Call of ABRAHAM, *and the Promises made to him.* Sodom *and* Gomorrah *destroyed.* Isaac *born.*

THREE hundred and fifty two years after the flood, and the next after *Noah's* death, the great patriarch *Abraham*

ham was born, the father of the *Jewish* nation, and (in a spiritual sense) of all the faithful; when he was seventyfive years of age, God was pleased to call him out of his native country to go into the land of *Canaan* which he promised to give to his descendants; that he would make of him *a great nation*, and that *in him should all the families of the earth be blessed*: As from him according to the flesh, should descend the *Messiah*, the Saviour of the world.

About the 27th year of his age, *Salem* (afterwards called *Jerusalem*) situated in the center of *Judea*, was built by *Melchisedeck*; and in the 99th year of *Abraham* the sacrament of circumcision was given to him and his posterity.

Now *Sodom* and *Gomorrah*, *Admah* and *Zeboim*, where for their abominable sins destroyed by fire and brimstone from heaven; only the righteous *Lot* with his wife and daughters, were brought out of it by two angels, whom *Lot* had entertained: But his wife for looking back

after

after her escape, was turned into a pillar of salt.

In *Abraham's* 100th year and *Sarah's* 90th, *Isaac* was born. Fifty years after which the patriarch *Shem* died, A. M. 2151. From thence it is evident, that the whole series of things, from the creation to this time, might be orally transmitted down in three lives only. For as *Isaac* was fifty years cotemporary with *Shem*, so *Shem*, was ninety seven with *Methuselah*, and he 244 with *Adam*. *Methuselah* died but the year before the deluge;

uge; and it is very natural to believe, that he discoursed often with his grandson *Noah* and his sons on the subjects of the creation and fall, as he had received the same from *Adam*. When *Isaac* was twentyfive years old, God, in trial of *Abraham's* faith and obedience, commanded him to offer up this his only son. The

good man without any hesitation, complied with the divine command; but just as he was about to slay *Isaac*, the angel of the Lord called him to resist; and *Abraham* looking about him saw a ram
caught

caught by the horns in a thicket, which he offered up instead of his son. *Abraham* having lived to the age of 175 years, gave up the ghost, and his sons *Isaac* and *Ishmael*, buried him in the cave of *Macpelah*, which he had purchased for a family sepulchre, and where he himself had buried *Sarah* his wife.

In the 60th year of *Isaac's* age *Jacob* was born, who was the father of *Joseph*, whose affecting history is the subject of the following chapter.

Of JOSEPH *and his Brethren.*

THE Patriarch *Joseph* had twelve sons, who were the heads of the twelve tribes or families of the children of *Israel*. Their names were *Reuben, Simeon, Levi, Judah, Issacher, Zebulon, Dan, Napthali, Gad, Asher, Joseph* and *Benjamin*. Of all these sons he had the greatest affection for *Joseph* and *Benjamin*, but the former was his peculiar favourite, and accordingly distinguished from the rest by gay and party coloured apparel. This raised the envy of his brethren; but what
increased

increased their disgust was, that *Joseph*, having always the ear of his indulgent father, was very officious in telling him their faults, or any little stories to their disadvantage. Thus he became the object of their mortal hatred; which was still more aggravated by his telling them two remarkable dreams; the one, that as they were binding sheaves in the field, his sheaf arose and stood in the midst of theirs, and that theirs made obeisance to his sheaf. The other, that the sun, moon, and eleven stars made obeisance to him. Both which seemed to portend his future advancement and grandeur, and their being obliged to bow down before him.

Hereupon they determined to destroy him; and having a favourable opportunity when they were feeding their father's flocks in a distant part of the country, they conspired together to kill him, and to report that some wild beast had devoured him, and then (said they in derision) *we shall see what will become of his dreams*. But *Reuben* dissuaded them

from

from their cruel purpose, saying to them, *shed no blood, but cast him into this pit in the wilderness*; intending afterwards privately to carry him to his father. Accordingly they cast him into the pit, as *Reuben* advised, having first stripped him

of his coat of many colours, and *sat down to eat bread*. Whilst they were thus regaling themselves, they espied a company of merchants advancing towards them, upon which they went and drew *Joseph* out of the pit, and sold him for twenty pieces of silver. This was done
in

in the abſence of *Reuben*, who returning to the pit, and not finding *Joſeph* there, rent his clothes, and coming to his brethren, cried out, *the child is not, and I, whither ſhall I go?* They then formed a ſcheme to conceal their guilt and deceive their aged father, to which purpoſe they killed a kid, and having dipped *Joſeph*'s coat in the blood, they carried it home to *Jacob*; upon the ſight of which the poor man, not ſuſpecting any fallacy, but concluded that his darling ſon was torn in pieces by wild beaſts, burſt into tears, and *mourned many days refuſing to be comforted*.

The merchants who had bought *Joſeph*, carried him to the court of *Pharaoh* king of *Egypt*, and there ſold him to *Potiphar*, a captain of the guards. This officer obſerving that *Joſeph* was very careful and induſtrious, and that every thing *proſpered in his hand*, advanced him to be ſteward over all his houſhold; and for *Joſeph*'s ſake *the bleſſing of the Lord was upon all that* Potiphar *had in the houſe, and in the field*.

Now

THE HOLY BIBLE.

Now *Joseph* being a very comely youth, his mistress was so charmed with his person, that she endeavoured, time after time, to allure him to her bed; but his

virtue was proof against all her amorous solicitation. Upon this unexpected coldness her love was turned to hatred; having falsely accused him to her husband of an insolent attempt to rob her of her honour, the too credulous *Potiphar*, without further enquiry, confined him in the king's prison.

Joseph had not been long there, before he

he gave such evidences of his wisdom and virtue, that the keeper treated him with great indulgence. He had a peculiar talent at interpreting dreams, of which the instances of *Pharoah*'s chief butler and baker are a sufficient proof; and in process of time he had an opportunity of shewing it to *Pharoah* himself, whose remarkable dreams concerning the fat and lean kine, and the full and thin ears of corn, gave him great uneasiness, none of his learned magicians being able to interpret them, or give him any satisfaction. This occasioned the chief butler to remember *Joseph*, and he recommended him to *Pharaoh*, who sent for him out of prison, and related to him his dreams. Having heard them, he assured the king, that the seven fat kine and the seven full ears of corn, denoted seven years of plenty; and the seven lean kine and the seven thin ears signified seven years of famine; advising him to fill all the store houses with corn during the first seven years, that he might supply the wants of his people during

the

the following years of scarcity, and thereby gain immense sums of money. In a word, *Joseph*'s scheme was highly approved of, and himself appointed to put it in execution, being made steward of *Pharaoh*'s household, and ruler (next to the King) *over all the land of Egypt*.

As *Joseph* had foretold, the seven years of plenty were followed by a severe famine, which extended as far as the land of *Canaan*, where *Jacob* lived; who, hearing of the store laid up in *Egypt*, sent all his sons thither (except *Benjamin*) to buy corn for their subsistence. When *Joseph* saw his brethren, he knew them, but *made himself strange, and spake roughly to them*, saying, *Whence come ye?* and they answered, *From the land of Canaan to buy food*, but he told them they were *spies* and were *come to see the nakedness of the land*. And they replied, *Nay, my Lord we are no spies; thy servants are twelve brethren, the sons of one man in the land of Canaan; and behold, the youngest is this day with our father, and one is not*. Well said *Joseph, hereby ye shall be* **proved**: *For by* the life of Pharaoh ye shall not go forth hence except your youngest brother come hither. Send one of you, and let him fetch your brother, and ye shall be kept in prison, that your words may be proved.* Having confined them for three days, he made them another proposal : *If ye be true men,* (said he) *let one of your brethren be bound in the house of our prison; and go ye, carry corn for the famine of your houses. But bring your youngest brother unto me; so shall your words be verified, and ye shall not die.* In this situation they began to reflect on their ill treatment of *Joseph,* saying, *We are very guilty concerning our brother in that when he besought us we would not hear; therefore is this distress come upon us.*

These **words** were spoken in the presence of Joseph, but his brethren knew not that he understood them ; for he conversed with them by an interpreter. *And he turned himself from them and wept; and* returning to them again, took *Simeon* and *bound him before their eyes.* He then gave orders to fill their sacks with corn, to put each man's money into his sack, and

THE HOLY BIBLE. 51

and to give them provisions for their journey. This done, they departed; and one of them on the road, having opened his sack to give his ass provender, espied his money, and shewed it to his brethren, at which they were very much surprised and frighted. However, they pursued their journey, and came to *Jacob*, and told him all that had befallen them; particularly that the Lord of the country has detained *Simeon* and insisted on their bringing their brother *Benjamin* into *Egypt*. This was malancholly news to the good old man, and drew from him this complaint; *Me have ye bereaved of my children; Joseph is not and Simeon is not, and ye will take Benjamin also.* To which he added, *My son shall not go with you, for if mischief befal him by the way, ye will bring down my grey hairs with sorrow to the grave.*

At length, however, when their corn was all consumed, and the famine was still sore in the land, *Jacob* was prevailed upon by *Judah's* promise to bring *Benjamin* safe home again, to let him go
down

down with his brethren into *Egypt*; and for fear it was owing to some mistake that they brought back the money in their sacks, he now ordered them to take double the quantity, together with a handsome present for the Lord of the country. As soon as *Joseph* was acquainted with their arrival, he ordered a dinner to be provided for them at his own house, and *Simeon* was released from his confinement. When *Joseph* came in they brought him their presents in the most submissive manner, *bowing themselves to the earth*; but he was so affected at the sight of *Benjamin*, that he retired into his chamber and wept. At dinner time he returned to them again; and having placed them according to seniority, he sent messes to each of them, but *Benjamin*'s mess was five times as big as any of the rest.

Joseph having thus entertained his brethren, commanded his steward to fill their sacks with corn, and put each man's money in his sack's mouth, and his silver cup into the sack belonging to *Benjamin*

jamin. In the morning they set out with their asses, but had not got far from the city, when a messenger overtook them, who accused them with stealing the cup. They all denied the charge, saying, *God forbid thy servants should do this thing;* and put the matter upon this issue, *With whomsoever of thy servants it be found, let him die, and we will be my Lord's bond-men.* Search being made, the cup was found in *Benjamin's sack;* whereupon *they rent their clothes, and returned to the city;* and being come to Joseph's house, *they fell down before him on the ground.* And Joseph said, *What deed is this that ye have done?* And Judah answered, *What shall we say unto our Lord, or how shall we clear ourselves? God hath found out our iniquity and we are thy* bondslaves. But Joseph replied, *God forbid! The man with whom the cup is found shall be my servant; but as for you, get you up in peace unto your father.* Then Judah represented to him with what difficulty he had persuaded *Jacob* to part with *Benjamin,* and that he was obliged to become
surety

surety for the lad to his father, saying, if I bring him not unto thee again, then will I bear the blame for ever. Therefore, I pray thee, let thy servant be a bond slave instead of the lad, and let him go up with his brethren; for how shall I go to my father, and the lad be not with me? If I do, he will surely die.

Joseph could now no longer refrain, but ordered every man out of the room before he made himself known to his brethren. And he wept aloud! And said, I am Joseph; doth my father yet live. At this they were astonished, and could not answer him, for they were troubled at his presence. He then desired them to come near to him, and said: I am Joseph, your brother whom ye sold into Egypt. Now therefore, be not grieved nor angry with yourselves that ye sold me hither; for it was not you that sent me, but God sent me before you to preserve life. Haste ye to my father and say unto him: Thus saith thy son Joseph, God hath made me Lord of all Egypt; come down unto me, tarry not: And thou shalt dwell in the land of Goshen, and there will I nourish thee

thee, lest thou and thy household come to poverty; for there are yet five years of famine. Behold your eyes see, and the eyes of my brother Benjamin, that it is my mouth that speaketh unto you. And he fell upon Benjamin's neck, and wept, and Benjamin wept upon his neck. Moreover he kissed all his brethren, and wept upon them; after which they talked freely together.

Pharaoh was pleased when he heard of this pathetick interview, and ordered *Joseph* to send waggons along with his brethren, to bring their father, their wives, and children into *Egypt*. And *Joseph* did so, giving them provisions for the way; and sent his father twenty asses laden with good things of the land. But when they came to *Jacob* and told him that *Joseph* was yet alive, and governour over all the land of *Egypt*, his *heart fainted, for he believed them not*. However, when he had heard the whole message, and saw the waggons that were sent to carry him down, his spirit revived and he said, *It is enough, Joseph my son is yet alive: I will go and see him before I die.*

So

So *Jacob* and all his family, set out for *Egypt*: And *Joseph* went in his chariot to meet his father, and fell on his neck, and wept greatly; and *Israel* said unto *Joseph, Now let me die, since I have seen thy face, and thou art yet alive, Oh my son!*

Chap. X.

The Oppression of the Children of Israel *in* Egypt, *and their Deliverance from thence.*

BY the express order of *Pharaoh*, the children of *Israel* (who were seventy in number) were seated in the land of *Goshen*, the most fertile part of *Egypt*; where the good Patriach *Jacob* lived seventeen years, and then died, at the age of a hundred and forty seven. His body being embalmed, was carried into the land of *Canaan* to be buried with his ancestors; *Joseph* and his brethren, with the servants of *Pharaoh*, the elders of his house, and the elders of the land of *Egypt*, attending the solemnity. *Joseph* died fifty eight years after his father, being a hundred and ten years old.

The *Israelites* now increased and multiplied so exceedingly, that *Pharaoh*, (a new King who knew not *Joseph*) being afraid they would grow too powerful, endeavoured to destroy them. With this view he set taskmasters over them, who "made their lives bitter with hard bondage, in mortar, and in brick, and in all manner of service in the field; but the more they were afflicted, the more they multiplied and grew." This rigorous treatment not having the intended effect, *Pharaoh* ordered the *Hebrew* midwives to kill all the male children of the *Israelites*, as soon as they were born; but the midwives disobeying this wicked command, he charged his own people to execute his cruel purpose, saying, "Every son that is born ye shall cast into the river, and every daughter ye shall save alive."

Now the wife of a certain *Levite* being delivered of a fine boy, she concealed him for three months; but finding she could not hide him any longer she put him into an ark of bulrushes, and laid him

him in the flags by the river's brink trusting the event to providence. In

this condition the babe was found by *Pharaoh*'s daughter, who took compassion on him, employed his own mother to nurse him and afterwards kept him as her own son giving him the name of *Moses*.

When the foundling, thus providentially preserved, was grown up to a state of manhood, " he went out to his brethren, and looked on their burthens," and seeing an *Egyptian* strike an *Hebrew*. he
killed

killed the *Egyptian*, and buried him in
the sand. This coming to the ears of
Pharaoh, *Moses* was obliged to fly into the
land of *Midian*, where he married; and
as he was keeping the flocks of *Jethro*
his fatherinlaw, God appeared to him
in a burning bush, told him he had seen
the afflictions of his people in *Egypt* and
sent him to be their deliverer. Accordingly he carried the divine message to
Pharaoh, and having (with his brother
Aaron) wrought many miracles, and
smote *Egypt* with ten plagues, he at
length forced the hardened king to let
the *Israelites* depart out of his territories.
This event happened 430 years after the
call of *Abraham*, 140 after *Joseph*'s death,
in the year of the world 2513, and 1491
years before *Jesus Christ*.

The evening before the departure of
the *Israelites*, the 14th day of the first
month, (the beginning of our *May*) God
instituted the feast of the Passover, or
eating the paschal lamb, to be kept year-
ly throughout their generations for ever,
in commemoration of his passing by, and

sparing

sparing the houses of the *Israelites*, when he destroyed all the first born of the *Egyptians*.

Some time whilst the *Israelites* were in bondage, lived *Job*, a man eminent for his patience under afflictions; the account whereof in the book that bears his name, is generally believed to have been written by *Moses*, though some ascribe it to *Elihu*.

Chap. XI.

Pharaoh *and his Host drowned in the Red Sea.——The Murmuring of the* Israelites.

SOON after the children of *Israel* were gone out of *Egypt*, *Pharaoh*'s heart was hardened, and he pursued them with his whole army; and coming up with them near the *Red Sea*, God was pleased to work their deliverance in a very wonderful manner, by dividing the sea, so that the *Israelites* walk through it on dry land, and the *Egyptians* that followed them were so totally overwhelmed by the return of the waters, that

that not one of the host of *Pharaoh* remained alive.

This miracle made an awful impression (as well it might) upon the minds of the *Israelites*, who thereupon *feared and believed the Lord, and his servant Moses*. But in a few days they began to shew a murmuring discontented spirit; first, at the bitter waters of *Marah*, which were miraculously made sweet; and then in the wilderness of *Sin*, where they complained for want of bread, wishing they had died in *Egypt*, when they *sat by*

the

The HISTORY of

the flesh pots, and did eat bread to the full. To satisfy their hunger, God was pleased to send a prodigious flight of quails, which covered their whole camp, and the next morning he rained manna from heaven, with which bread he fed them during their forty years passage through the wilderness.

After such signal instances of the goodness of the Almighty towards them, one would imagine it impossible the *Israelites* should ever distrust his providence again: And yet in a short time, when they were encamped at *Rephidim*

and

and found no water, they murmured against *Moses*, and were *almost ready to stone him*. Hereupon God commanded *Moses* to take his rod, and smite the rock in *Horeb*, which he did in the sight of the people, and the water gushed out abundantly.

CHAP. XII.

The LAW *published on Mount* Sinai.

FIFTY days after the departure of the *Israelites* out of *Egypt*, whilst they were encamped near *Mount Sinai*, God

called

called *Moses* to the top of the *Mount*; and there, with the most awful solemnity of thunder, lightning, and the voice of the trumpet, (which made all the people in the camp tremble) delivered to him the ten commandments of the law, written upon two tables of stone.* The four first commandments, which make the *first table*, having an immediate respect to God himself; and the six last commandments, which make the *second table* comprise with the several branches of duty to our neighbour. They are here inserted, from the twentieth chapter of Exodous.

* It may not be improper to observe here, that the *patriarchal state* commenced from the beginning of the world, and continued until this delivery of the law. There were reckoned ten Patriarchs before the flood, viz. *Adam, Seth, Enos, Cainan, Mahalaleel, Jared, Enoch Methuselah, Lamech Land Noah.* The Patriarchs after the flood, were *Shem, Arphaxad, Selar, Heber, Peleg, Reu, Serug Nahor, Terah, Abraham, Isaac* and *Jacob*: who with Jacob's twelve sons, (more commonly distinguished by the name of Patriarchs) make in all thirty four.

TABLE

Table I.

I. Thou shalt have no other Gods but me.

II. Thou shalt not make to thyself any graven image, nor the likeness of any thing that is in heaven above, or in the earth beneath, or in the water under the earth. Thou shalt not bow down to them, nor worship them: For I the Lord thy God am a jealous God, and visit the sins of the fathers upon the children unto the third and fourth generation of them that hate me; and shew mercy unto thousands of them that love me, and keep my commandments.

III. Thou shalt not take the name of the Lord thy God in vain: For the Lord will not hold him guiltless that taketh his name in vain.

IV. Remember that thou keep holy the Sabbath day. Six days shalt thou labour, and do all that thou hast to do; but the seventh day is the sabbath of the Lord thy God: In it thou shalt do no manner of work, thou, and thy son, and thy

thy daughter, and thy man-servant, and thy maid-servant, thy cattle, and the stranger that is within thy gates: For in six days the Lord made heaven and earth, the sea, and all that in them is, and rested the seventh day: Wherefore the Lord blessed the seventh day, and hallowed it.

Table II.

V. Honour thy father and thy mother, that thy days may be long in the land which the Lord thy God giveth thee.

VI. Thou shalt do no murder.

VII. Thou shalt not commit adultery.

VIII. Thou shalt not steal.

IX. Thou shalt not bear false witness against thy neighbour.

X. Thou shalt not covet thy neighbour's house, thou shalt not covet thy neighbour's wife, nor his servant, nor his maid, nor his ox, nor his ass, nor any thing that is his.

The year after the giving of the law, God commanded the *tabernacle* to be erected, and sacrifices to be offered by the priests

priests upon the altar; and appointed *Aaron* and his sons to be set apart and consecrated to minister before him in the priest's office. The ceremonial law was also given; and the holy utensils, the priests' habits and all things belonging to the *Levitical* service, were settled and regulated.

The tabernacles consisted of two parts, the *Holy of Holies*, and the *Holy Places*. Into the *Holy of Holies*, which was without the veil, where stood the *ark* covered with the *mercy seat*, none might enter but the high priest, once a year, upon the great day of expiation, when he made an atonement for the sins of the people by sprinkling blood. In the *Holy Place*, without the veil, stood the *golden candlestick*, the *altar of incense*, and the *table of shewbread*. And in the court of the tabernacle stood the *brazen altar* and the *laver*.———But, for a particular account of what relates to the *ceremonial* as well as *political* laws which the *Israelites* were to observe, we must refer to the books of *Moses* themselves.

CHAP. XIII.

Of the BRAZEN SERPENT.—*The Story of* BALAAM *and his* ASS.

WE shall not follow the *Israelites* from Mount *Sinai* through the various journies and encampments in the wilderness, but bring them at once towards the borders of the *promised land*. And even here, after they had been for so many years miraculously nourished and preserved, they could not forbear giving a fresh instance of their murmuring and perverse dispositions: For in *Punon*, (their 35th encampment) they loathed their manna, and *spake against God and against Moses, wherefore have ye brough us up out of Egypt to die in the wilderness; for there is no bread, neither is there any water.* Numb. xxi. 5. This provoked the Lord to send fiery serpents among them, and they bit the people, so that great numbers of them died; whereupon they besought *Moses* to intercede for them, that the fiery serpents might be taken away.

THE HOLY BIBLE. 69

way. And God commanded *Moses* to make a serpent of brass, and put it upon a pole; which being done, whoever was bitten by a fiery serpent, when *he beheld the serpent of brass, he lived.* The brazen

serpent by looking upon which the *Israelites* were healed, was a lively type of *Christ* upon the cross; by looking up to whom with an eye of faith, the wounded sinner is saved from that death which he must otherwise inevitably suffer.

In a few more journies the *Israelites* arrived at the plains of *Moab*, where they

they encamped, on this side the river *Jordan*, near *Jericho*. Their numbers, and their conquests of the *Amorites*, gave *Balak*, king of the *Moabites*, very uneasy apprehensions for his own dominions. Hereupon he sent for *Balaam* to come and curse the *Israelites*, not doubting but he might then attack them with success, and drive them out of his territories. But God commanded *Balaam* not to go along with the messengers, nor to curse *Israel*, whom he himself had blessed. *Balak*, however, sent a second message to *Balaam*, promising him great honours and rewards, if he would come and do what he desired. With these messengers God permitted him to go, but with this command, *the word which I shall say unto thee, that shalt thou do.* Upon this *Balaam* saddled his ass, and set out with the messengers; but as he was riding along, the angel of the Lord stood in his way with a drawn sword in his hand: Which the ass perceiving, turned aside, and *Balaam* smote her to keep her in the road. A second time, the

angel

THE HOLY BIBLE. 7

angel standing in a path between two walls, the afs gave way, and crushed *Balaam's* foot against the wall; and he fmote her again. The third time, the afs faw the angel in a narrow way, where there was no room to turn either to the right or to the left; and then fhe fell down under *Balaam*, who was thereupon fo enraged, that he fmote her more feverely than before. Then the Lord opened the mouth of the afs, and fhe faid unto *Balaam, what have I done unto thee, that thou haft fmitten me thefe three times?*

times? And *Balaam* said unto the ass, *behold thou hast mocked me: I would there were a sword in mine hand, for now would I kill thee.* And the ass said unto *Balaam, Am not I thine ass, upon which thou hast ridden ever since I was thine, unto this day? was I ever wont to do so unto thee?* And he said, *nay.* Then the Lord opened the eyes of Balaam, and he saw the angel with his sword drawn in his hand, and he bowed down his head, and fell flat on his face, acknowledging that he had sinned; upon which the angel permitted him to proceed on his journey.

CHAP. XIV.

The Israelites *pass through* Jordan, *and take* Jericho. *The Sun and Moon stand still. The History of* SAMSON. SAUL *anointed King. The story of* DAVID *and* GOLIAH *The Reign of* DAVID.

IN the 36th year of the *Israelites'* sojourning in the wilderness, *Aaron* died, and was succeeded in the High Priesthood by his son *Eleazer*. The next day died *Moses*, having had a view of the
promised

promised land from Mount *Nebo*, and was succeeded by *Joshua* in the civil government.

In the year before *Christ* 1451, (to which era the following dates have respect) *Joshua* conducted the *Israelites* through the river *Jordan* into *Canaan*; the waters thereof being miraculously divided (like those of the *Red Sea*) to afford them a passage on dry land. The next day circumcision was renewed, which ceremony had been omitted during their forty years abode in the wilderness. Soon after (when they began to eat the corn of the land) manna ceased.

The inhabitants of *Canaan* were now to be conquered and destroyed by the *Israelites*, that they themselves might possess the country, according to the divine promise. *Jericho* was the first obstacle they met with; and God, being willing to shew them that they should not depend upon their own strength for victory, commanded the ark of the covenant to be carried seven times round the city, preceded by seven priests blowing

ing trumpets of ram's horns; and the seventh time, upon the particular signal, the people were ordered to give a loud shout, at which the walls of *Jericho* fell down to the ground, and the *Israelites* entered the city, and put to the sword men, women, and children, sparing only the harlot *Rahab* and her family, according to the promise of the spies, whom she had concealed and saved from falling into the hands of their pursuers.

The city of *Ai* was soon after taken by stratagem; and the *Gibeonites* having artfully

THE **HOLY BIBLE**. 75

artfully made a league with the *Ifraelites* five kings joined their forces to befiege *Gibeon*. Hereupon Jofhua marched to the relief of the *Gibeonites*; and falling unexpectedly on the confederate army, he made a great flaughter, and put the reft to flight. Many were flain in the purfuit, but a fhower of large hailftones deftroyed more than the fword; and, at the prayer of *Jofhua*, the fun and moon ftood ftill, until the *Ifraelites* had completed their victory, and fully avenged themfelves upon their enemies. The

five

five kings escaped, and hid themselves in a cave; but being discovered, they were brought out and hanged, and their bodies thrown into the cave where they had taken refuge.

Joshua, pursuing his victories, subdued many other kings and nations, and divided the promised land among the children of *Israel*. In 1444 the tabernacle was set up at *Shiloh*; and in 1427 Joshua died, having governed *Israel* four and twenty years.

After the death of *Joshua*, the *Israelites* were governed by judges, whom God raised up from time to time to deliver them from their enemies. This kind of government began in the year 1405, and continued until *Saul* was anointed king over *Israel*. The names of the judges were, 1. *Othniel*; 2. *Ehud*; 3. *Deborah* and *Barak*; 4. *Gideon*; 5. *Abimelech*; 6. *Tolah*; 7. *Jair*; 8. *Jephthah*; 9. *Ibzan*; 10. *Elon*; 11. *Abdon*; 12. *Samson*; 13. *Eli*; 14. *Samuel*. Of these the most remarkable for their exploits were *Gideon* and *Samson*; the former of whom

whom, with only three hundred chosen men, (according to God's appointment) destroyed a numerous army of *Midianites*, together with their kings and princes, and thereby entirely delivered *Israel* from their oppressive yoke.

Samson the son of *Manoah*, was born at the time the *Philistines* had dominion over *Israel*, being ordained by God to *begin their deliverance*, according to the prediction of the angel to his mother, *Judges* xiii. 5. When he was grown up to manhood, he cast his eyes on one of the daughters of the *Philistines* at *Timnath*, and desired his father and mother to procure her for his wife. His parents at first objected to his choice, as being a *Philistine* : but finding him insist upon it, they agreed to accompany him to *Timnath*. In their way thither, when *Samson* was at some distance from them, *a young lion roared against him. And the spirit of the Lord came mightily upon him, and he rent him as he would have rent a kid, and he had nothing in his hand* ; *but he told not his*

78 THE HISTORY OF

his father and mother what he had done. So they proceeded on their journey to *Timnath*, and the proposed marriage was agreed on by all parties.

After some time, when *Samson* returned to marry his wife, he found a swarm of bees and honey in the carcase of the dead lion; and at his wedding feast he propounded this riddle to thirty young men at the table, viz. *Out of the eater came forth meat, and out of the strong came forth sweetness*; promising them thirty changes of raiment if they could explain it within seven days; and if they could not, they were to make him the same present. The fixed time being almost elapsed, *Samson*'s wife prevailed on him to reveal the secret to her, which she immediately communicated to her countrymen. This so enraged *Samson*, that he slew thirty *Philistines*, and gave their garments to those who had expounded the riddle.

Samson being afterwards denied his wife, whom her father had given to another man, resented it so highly, that he caught three hundred foxes, and having tied them tail to tail, with firebrands between each, he let them loose among the standing corn of the *Philistines*, whereby it was burnt up, together with the vineyards and olives. This enraged the *Philistines* to such a degree, that they burnt his wife and his father; which cruelty *Samson* revenged, by making a great slaughter amongst them.

These mutual acts of hostility occasioned the *Philistines* to assembly an army against the men of *Judah*, who, dreading their

THE HISTORY OF

their refentment, perfuaded *Samfon* to let them bind him with new cords, and deliver him into their hands. This being done, his enemies feeing him bound gave a great fhout; on which the fpirit of the Lord coming upon *Samfon*, and he fnapped the cords as if they had been *burnt flax*, and finding the jaw bone of an afs, he fell upon the *Philiftines*, and therewith flew a thoufand men.

Samfon's carrying away the gates of *Gaza*, when the inhabitants had fhut him in in, with an intent to kill him, was another instance of his surprising strength; of which, however, he was at length deprived by the cunning and treachery of *Delilah*, and so became a prey to his mortal enemies. The Lords of the *Philistines* applied themselves to this prostitute, for whom they knew *Samson* had a great affection, offering her large rewards if she cou'd prevail upon him to tell her where his extraordinary strength lay. Three several times he amused her with wrong accounts, and thereby escaped the snare into which she would have drawn him; but at last, quite tired with her repeated solicitations, he told her all his heart: *There has not come a razor upon mine head; but if I be shaven, then my strength will go from me, and I shall become weak, and be like any other man.* Hereupon Delilah, having lulled him to sleep upon her knees caused the *seven locks of his head* to be shaven off, *and his strength went from him*; and then giving notice to the *Philistines*, they seized him, put out his eyes

The HISTORY of

eyes, carried him to *Gaza*, and there bound him with fetters of brass, and he did grind in the prison house.

In a little time, as *Sampson*'s hair began to grow again, his strength also returned, which he had soon an opportunity of exerting to the destruction of his enemies: For the Lords of the *Philistines* being assembled to offer sacrifice to their God *Dagon* for having delivered *Samson* into their hands, when their hearts were merry they sent for him out of prison to make them sport, placing him between

the

the two pillars that supported the temple; which *Samson* perceiving, he took hold of them, one with his right hand and the other with his left; and called upon God to assist him that once to be avenged of the *Philistines* for the loss of his eyes, and desiring to die with them, " he bowed himself with all his might, and the house fell upon the Lords, and upon all the people therein: So the dead which he slew at his death were more than they which he slew in his life."

Next after *Samson*, the High priest *Eli* became Judge of *Israel*; in whose days *Samuel* was born, and called to be a prophet of the Lord. During *Eli*'s administration, the *Israelites* were overcome by the *Philistines*, who in one battle killed thirty thousand of them (*Eli*'s two sons being among the slain) and carried away the ark of the covenant; which melancholly news being brought to *Eli*, he fell backward from his seat and broke his neck, after he had judged *Israel* forty years.

Under

Under his successor *Samuel*, the *Philistines* were subdued, the cities they had taken were restored, and the *Israelites* were happy during his wise and just administration. But *Samuel* growing old, and entrusting the government to his sons, they "walked not in their father's way, but turned after lucre, took bribes, and perverted judgment. Hereupon the people grew dissatisfied, and desired *Samuel* to make them a king to judge them like other nations, to go out before them and to fight their battles. This displeased *Samuel*, and he prayed unto the Lord; who commanded him to comply with their request: And accordingly, by divine appointment, (in the year 1095) he anointed *Saul* king of *Israel*.

So long as *Saul* continued obedient to the commands of God by his prophet *Samuel*, success attended his arms, and his enemies fell before him; but at last, being ordered utterly to destroy the *Amalekites* together with their cattle, and having spared *Agag* their king, and some of the best of their sheep and oxen, God
was

was so provoked at his disobedience, that he determined to transfer the kingdom from him to *David*; to anoint whom (in the year 1063) *Samuel* was sent to *Bethlehem*.

At this juncture an occasion offered to signalize *David's* valour in the face of all *Israel*: For *Saul* being at war with the *Philistines*, and both armies lying incamped near each other, there came forth a champion from the camp of the *Philistines* of a gigantick stature and prodigious strength, who for forty days together bid defiance to the whole army of the *Israelites*, challenging them to send out a man to fight him, and put an end to the war by single combat. The name of this mighty giant was *Goliah*, whose bulk and aspect struck such a terror into the *Israelites*, that they fled whenever he appeared.

Now it happened that *David*, who kept his father's sheep, was sent to the camp with provisions for his three brethren, then in the service of *Saul*; and finding what a panick run through the army,

army, and that the king had offered to give his own daughter to the man that should kill the monstrous *Goliah*, he expressed his inclination to engage this terrible adversary. Hereupon his eldest brother was very angry with him, accusing him of *pride and haughtiness of heart*, and of neglecting his proper business, the care of his *few sheep in the wilderness*. *David*, however, was not discouraged by this rebuke; but talking to other persons on the same subject, he was at length taken notice of, and introduced to *Saul*; who perceiving that he was but a mere stripling, represented to him how unequal a match he was for a man of *Goliah*'s strength and military experience. To obviate this objection, *David* said to the king, *thy servant kept his father's sheep, and there came a lion and a bear, and took a lamb out of the flock; and thy servant slew both the lion and the bear: And this Philistine shall be as one of them, seeing he has defied the armies of the living God:* adding, to
shew

THE HOLY BIBLE. 87

shew that his trust and confidence was in God alone, *the Lord that delivered me out of the paw of the lion and out of the paw of the bear, he will deliver me out of the hand of this Philistine.*

Saul animated with *David*'s story and resolution, ordered his own armour to be put upon him; which being undoubtedly too heavy for *David*, and his dependance being solely upon the divine assistance, he put it off again, chusing to meet

the giant with only his sling and his staff.

When *Goliah* saw *David* advance to him thus accoutred, he curſed him by his vain Gods, and ſaid, *am I a dog, that thou comeſt to me with ſtaves? Come hither, and I will give thy fleſh unto the fowls of the air, and to the beaſts of the field.* Then ſaid *David* to the *Philiſtine, thou comeſt to me with a ſword, and with a ſpear, and with a ſhield; but I come to thee in the name of the Lord of Hoſts, the God of the armies of Iſrael, whom thou haſt defied.* And when the *Philiſtine* drew nigh, *David* put his hand in his bag, took from thence a ſtone and flang it, and ſmote the *Philiſtine* on his forehead, ſo that he fell upon his face to the earth. Thus *David* prevailed on the *Philiſtine* with a fling and a ſtone, and ran and ſtood upon him, and ſlew him with his own ſword, and cut off his head. And when the *Philiſtines* ſaw their champion was killed, they fled; and the *Iſraelites* purſued them, and obtained a complete victory.

The ſucceſs attending this hazardous exploit, having gained *David* the applauſe and affection of the people, *Saul* grew

grew jealous of him, and determined to destroy him: But *Jonathan*, the son of *Saul*, was so sensible of his great merit, that he *loved him as his own soul*, and gave him notice from time to time of all the evil intended against him by his father. However, to avoid *Saul's* resentment, *David* was obliged to fly into the *wilderness*; whither *Saul* pursued him in vain, the Almighty being his protector. —Whilst affairs were in this situation the prophet *Samuel* died.

The Lord having now forsaken *Saul*, and his army being entirely routed by the *Philistines*, his three sons slain, and himself wounded; in these desperate circumstances he put an end to his life by falling on his own sword, and his armourbearer followed his example. This melancholy news greatly affected *David*, as appears by his pathetick lamentation for the loss of *Saul*, and more especially of *Jonathan* his beloved friend, 2. *Sam.* 1.

After this deplorable fate of *Saul* and his family, God was pleased to establish
the

the throne of *David* over *Israel* and *Judah*. He was a prince of extraordinary valour and wisdom, a prophet, and an excellent poet, the greatest part of the *Psalms* being of his composing. He subdued the *Philistines*, the *Moabites*, the *Syrians*, and other nations; and defeated some dangerous conspiracies that were formed against him, particularly that of his own son *Absalom*; for his rebellious force were routed by those of *David* in the wood of *Ephraim*, and *Absalom*'s hair

being entangled in the bough of an oak,
his

his mule went from under him, and left him hanging on the tree, where he was afterwards killed by *Joab*. In a word, having reigned forty years, and triumphed over his foreign and domestick enemies, he died in a good old age, leaving his crown and kingdom to his son *Solomon*.

Chap. XV.

Solomon's *Wisdom. His judgment between the two Harlots. The Building and Dedication of the Temple. History of the Prophets* Elijah *and* Elisha. Jezebel *eaten by dogs.*

IN the year before *Christ* 1015, *Solomon* ascended the throne of *Israel*; to whom, according to his request, God was pleased to grant such a degree of wisdom, that *there was none like him either before or after him*; and also made him superior in riches and honour, to all his predecessors or succeeding princes. It happened that

that an opportunity soon offered of shewing his extraordinary understanding and judgment, which gained him great reputation; for two harlots, who lived in one house by themselves, being brought to bed within three days of each other, the child of one of them dying, the mother changed the dead one for the live one, while the other was asleep, and insisted strongly that it was her own. The case being brought before *Solomon*, and both the women claimed the living child he ordered it to be divided between them with

a sword: To which the pretended mother assenting, the real one desired the king to let the other have it whole, rather than see her infant destroyed. From this natural tenderness, *Solomon* rightly judging her to be the true mother of the child, ordered it to be delivered to her accordingly.

The Almighty having reserved to the peaceable reign of *Solomon* the building a temple to his name, that prince began the important work in the year of the world 2992, 480 years after the departure of the *Israelites* out of *Egypt*, and 1010 before the coming of *Christ*. In this great undertaking he was assisted by *Hiram* king of *Tyre*, his father's ancient friend, who sent him vast quantities of cedar and other timber for that purpose. In a word, he erected a most stately fabrick, and embellished it with variety of fine carved work, profusely overlaid with gold: But for its dimensions, curious workmanship, and the richness of its utensils and ornaments, we must refer to the account given of it in the holy scripture

94 THE HISTORY OF

Scripture (1 *Kings* vi. vii.) not having room in this small history to describe its

wonderful splendor, beauty and magnificence.

Solomon, having finished this glorious structure, summoned together a numerous assembly of *Israelites*, and caused the ark of the Lord to be carried into an apartment peculiarly allotted for its reception, by far the most rich and splendid of the whole building, called the *Holy of Holies* ; and then, with the utmost

most solemnity of prayer and sacrifice, dedicated the Temple to the only true God; and having made a feast for all *Israel*, which lasted fourteen days, he dismissed them *joyful and glad of heart.*

This great and wise prince, after a glorious reign of forty years, was succeeded (in the year before Christ 975) by his son *Reboboam!* through whose folly ten tribes of *Israel* revolted to *Jeroboam*, and himself ruled over two tribes only, which were those of *Judah* and *Benjamin*. Thus there were two kingdoms formed; the one called the *Kingdom of* ISRAEL, which comprehended the ten revolted tribes; the other called the *Kingdom of* JUDAH, which consisted of the two tribes that remained faithful to *Reboboam*.

The new king of *Israel*, fearing that his subjects would return to the obedience of *Reboboam* king of *Judah*, if they should go to *Jerusalem* to worship God in the Temple, and to offer their sacrifices there, set up two golden calves, and prevailed with the people to worship them

them under the name of the God of *Israel*; so that in the reign of *Jeroboam* idolatry was established, and in his successors kept up the same false worship. However, it pleased God to send several prophets to the ten tribes, to turn them from their sins, and to preserve the knowledge of himself amongst them. The most eminent of these prophets was *Elijah*, who prophesied against *Ahab* the wickedest of the kings of *Israel*; assuring him, that for some years to come there should be neither dew nor rain in the land.

In

In this time of drought, and of the famine consequent thereupon, God commanded *Elijah* to hide himself by the brook *Cherith*, and caused the ravens to bring him bread and flesh every morning and evening; and he drank of the brook, until at length it was quite dried up for want of rain.

Afterwards, by the divine command, *Elijah* went to a widow at *Zarephath*, whom he found gathering sticks, and desired her to fetch him a little bread and water; upon which the poor woman told him her distress; *I have not a cake,* (said she) *but a handful of meal in a barrel, and a little oil in a cruse; and behold, I am gathering sticks to make a fire to dress it for me and my son, that we may eat it and die.* Notwithstanding this, the prophet ordered her to bring him a little cake; and promised her, that her barrel of meal and cruse of oil should not fail, until the Lord sent rain upon the earth: Which was accordingly fulfilled.

Whilst *Elijah* sojourned with the widow, her son died; and God was pleased, ed, at the supplication of the prophet, to restore him to life, to the great joy of his mother, who at first was ready to impute his death to the presence of *Elijah*; but on seeing him alive again, *Now by this I know* (said she) *that thou art a man of God and that the word of the Lord in thy mouth is truth.*

When the drought had continued several years, and the famine raged in *Samaria*, God commanded *Elijah* to go and shew himself to *Ahab*, promising to send rain upon the earth; which he did abundantly, at the prayer of the prophet upon the earth; which he did abundantly, at the prayer of the prophet upon mount *Carmel*. Soon after this, his life being threatened by *Jezebel*, *Ahab*'s wife, because he had destroyed the prophets of *Baal*, he retired into the wilderness, where the Lord appeared to him, and ordered him, to anoint *Elisha* to succeed him as a prophet. *Elijah* having found *Elisha*, at plough, threw his mantle over him; and *Elisha* taking leave of his father and mother, followed *Elijah*.

About

THE HOLY BIBLE.

99

About the year 896, the two prophets came together to the river *Jordan*, the waters thereof *Elijah* smote with his mantle, *and they were divided hither and thither, so that they went both over on dry ground.* Now *Elijah* being sensible of his approaching removal, asked *Elisha* what he should do for him before he was taken away: To which *Elisha* answered, *let a double portion of thy spirit be upon me.* And as they went on and talked, *there apppeared a chariot of fire, and horses of fire, and*

parted them asunder, and Elijah went up by

by a whirlwind into heaven. When he was out of sight, *Elisha* took up the mantle that fell from him, and returned to *Jordan*, he divided the waters with it, and passed over on dry land as before.

It soon appeared that the spirit of *Elijah* rested on *Elisha*, and the miracles that he wrought gained him great esteem, and reputation. Now there came a certain woman to *Elisha*, saying, *thy servant my husband is dead, and thou knowest that thy servant did fear the Lord; and the*

creditor is come to take upon him my two sons to

to be bondsmen. And Elisha said unto her, what shall I do for thee? tell me what hast thou in the house? And she said, thine handmaid hath not any thing in the house, save a pot of oil. He then commanded her to borrow a great number of vessels of her neighbours, and pour into them until they were full, which she did accordingly; and found such a vast increase of her oil, that she sold part of it to discharge her debt, and had enough left for the subsistence of herself and her children.

After this *Elisha* restored the *Shunamite's* son to life, cured *Naaman* of his leprosy by sending him to wash in *Jordan*, smote *Gehazi* with the same distemper, caused iron to swim, and wrought many other miracles. In the year 884, he sent a young prophet to anoint *Jehu* king over *Israel*, and to declare to him the will of God that the whole family of *Ahab* should be destroyed. Whereupon *Jehu* being proclaimed by the soldiers, and having killed king *Joram*, *Ahab's* son, entered *Jezreel* in triumph, and seeing

ing the wicked *Jezebel* looking out of the palace window, he ordered her to be thrown down, and *some of her blood was sprinkled on the wall*, and the dogs afterwards devoured her body, (agreeable to

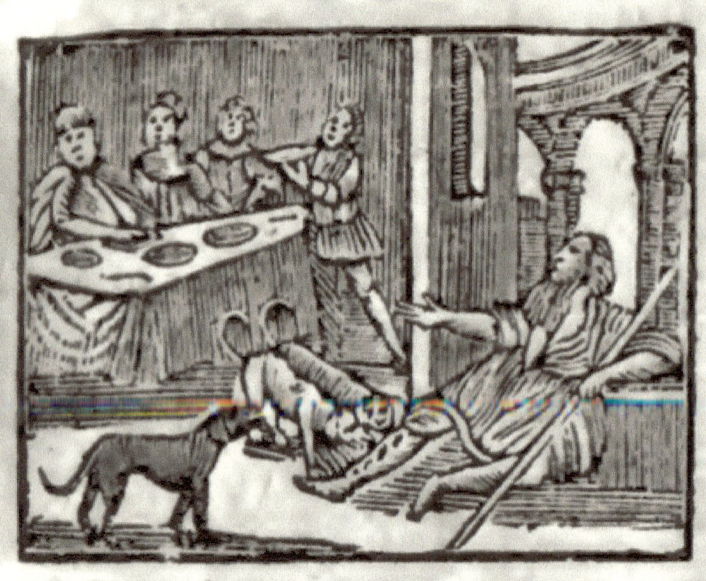

the prediction of the prophet *Elijah*) as a punishment for her wickedness, particularly the murder of *Naboth*.

CHAP.

CHAP. XVI.

JONAH *in the Whale's Belly*, SHADRACH, MESHACH *and* ABEDNEGO, *cast into a fiery Furnace.* DANIEL *in the Lion's Den. The* JEWISH *History brought down to the Birth of* CHRIST.

IN the reign of *Jehoash*, king of *Judah*, about the year before *Christ* 826 (or, according to others, in the reigns of *Azariah* king of *Judah*, and *Jeroboam* II. king of *Israel*, about the year 808) God commanded the prophet *Jonah* to go to *Ninevah*, the chief city of the *Assyrians*, and proclaim to its wicked inhabitants their approaching destruction: But instead of obeying the voice of the Lord, *Jonah* went down to *Joppa*, and there took shipping for *Tarshish*. Hereupon it pleased God to send a great storm, and *there was a mighty tempest in the sea*, which exceedingly terrified the mariners, who expected to perish every moment. In this danger they agreed to cast lots, to *know for whose cause the evil was come upon*

THE HISTORY OF

on them; and the lot fell upon Jonah. The prophet then ingenuously acknowledged that himself was the occasion of their distress, and desired them to throw him overboard; which they did, though not without much reluctance, *and the sea ceased from her raging. Now the Lord had prepared a great fish to swallow up Jonah, and he was in the belly of the fish three days and three nights;* in which dismal situation, he sincerely repented, and prayed the Lord; who thereupon caused the

fish to cast up Jonah *on the dry land.*
After

After this deliverance the prophet obeyed the divine command went to *Nineveh* and denounced its overthrow; but the *Ninevites* repenting in sackcloth and ashes, and turning from their evil ways, God was pleased to spare that great city, in which were *more than six score thousand persons that could not discern between their right hand and their left.*

In the year 788, in the reign of *Azariah*, or, *Uzziah*, king of *Judah*, *Amos* prophesied; and probably *Joel* prophesied in the same reign. In his reign likewise, and in those of *Jotham*, *Ahaz* and *Hezekiah*, lived the prophets *Isaiah*, *Hosea*, and *Micah*.

In the fifth year of *Hezekiah*, king of *Judah*, and the ninth of *Hoshea* king of *Israel* (before *Christ* 721) *Shalmanezer* king of *Assyria*, took *Samaria*, and carried the ten tribes captive into his own kingdom, from whence they were dispersed into divers countries, and have never since been settled in their own land. Thus ended the kingdom of *Israel*, after it had subsisted, separate from that of *Judah*

Judah, 254 years, under twenty kings of ten several families. In *Hezekiah's* reign *Nahum* prophesied.

In 599 *Jehoiakim* king of *Judah*, surrendered *Jerusalem* to *Nebuchadnezzar*, who carried him and the chief of the people captive to *Babylon*: And in 588, the eleventh year of *Zedekiah* (who succeeded *Jehoiakim*) *Nebuchadnezzar* took *Jerusalem* after a long siege, burnt the temple and the whole city, razed the walls and carried away the *Jews* into captivity. Thus was the kingdom of *Judah* destroyed, 468 years after the beginning of *David's* reign, 388 years from the division of the tribes, and 134 years after the destruction of the kingdom of *Israel*. *Obadiah* prophesied under *Zedekiah*.

Jeremiah and *Zephaniah* were cotemporaries; the former of whom prophesied fortyfive years, *viz.* from the 13th of *Josiah*, to the 5th of the *Babylonish* captivity. *Habakkuk* is also supposed to have prophesied in the reign of *Josiah*.

Ezekiel

Ezekiel who was carried away captive with *Jehoiakim* to *Babylon*, began to prophesy in the fifth year of his captivity; And *Daniel*, who was carried to *Babylon* in his youth, in the third year of *Jehoiakim* (607) prophesied there to the year 534, in all 73 years, and lived to be about the age of 94.

Whilst *Daniel* was a captive at *Babylon*, God was pleased to give him an extraordinary degree of wisdom, and he had *understanding in dreams and visions* far superior to all the magicians and astrologers of that kingdom. This was a mean of his advancement to great honour; for *Nebuchadnezzar* having forgot one of his dreams, which troubled him very much, and consulted his magicians to no purpose, ordered all the wise men of *Babylon* to be put to death. But *Daniel* desiring a little time to consider of it, the Lord *revealed the secret to him in a night vision*; and being brought before the king, he related to him his dream, and explained its meaning; whereupon *Nebuchadnezzar* made him great presents. and appointed him

him ruler over the province of *Babylon*. At *Daniel*'s request, his three fellow captives, *Shadrach*, *Meshach*, and *Abednego*, were also entrusted with the affairs of the kingdom.

These three *Jews* (whose real names were *Hannaniah*, *Mishael*, and *Azariah*) having absolutely refused to worship a golden image that *Nebuchadrezzar* had set up, he was so enraged against them, that he ordered them to be cast into a fiery furnace, heated seven times hotter than usual. The king's command was obeyed; but the most high God, whom they feared and worshipped, was with them and preserved them in the midst of the fire, and they came out of the furnace without *a hair of their heads singed, neither were their coats changed, nor had the smell of fire passed on them.*

This wonderful deliverance extorted from *Nebuchadnezzar*, who was an eye witness of it, an acknowledgment of the power of the God of *Israel*, but some years after, being proud of his victories, and boasting of the magnificence of his
buildings

buildings, he fell distracted, and (as *Daniel* had foretold when he interpreted another of his dreams) he *was driven from the society of men, and did eat grass as oxen, and his body was wet with the dew of heaven, until his hair was grown like eagle's feathers, and his nails like bird's claws.* After seven years thus spent among the beasts of the field, his reason returned to him, and he was restored to his kingdom, praising and honouring the King of heaven, *all whose works are truth, and his ways judgment, and those that walk in pride he is able to abase.*

In the year 538, *Belshazzar* king of *Babylon* made a great feast for his nobles, and caused the vessels of the house of the Lord to be fetched that *Nebuchadnezzar* his grandfather had brought from *Jerusalem*, out of which he himself, his princes, his wives and concubines drank wine to the glory of his idols, and the dishonour of the true God. But in the midst of his jollity, a hand appeared, and wrote on
the

the plaister of the wall, MENE MENE, TEKEL, UPHARSIN; which the king observing, he was greatly terrified, and sent for his *Chaldean* astrologers and magicians to read the writing, and give him the interpretation of it; but they not being able to do either, *Daniel* was called, who read and interpreted the writing; whereupon he was publickly proclaimed the third ruler in the kingdom. The same night *Belshazzar* was slain; and the *Assyrian* monarchy which had stood from its foundation by *Nimrod*, 1650 years,

years, was seized by *Darius* the *Mede*, and the *Persian* monarchy founded by *Cyrus*.

Daniel's greatness under *Darius* raising envy in some of the principal courtiers and officers they contrived his ruin, but finding nothing to accuse him of with respect to his management of publick affairs, they persuaded the king to sign a decree, that for thirty days no petition should be made to any God or man, but to himself only. This command *Daniel* disobeyed, by making supplication to his God as usual, and for so doing he was

cast

cast into a den of lions; but the king himself going to the den the next morning, and finding that *Daniel* had received no hurt, he caused his accusers to be cast into the same den, whom the lions presently devoured. And he published a decree, that all persons throughout his dominions should reverence and fear the God of *Daniel*.

The *Babylonish* captivity lasted seventy years, according to *Jeremiah's* prediction; which time being expired, *Cyrus* king of *Persia* gave the *Jews* leave, in the year 536) to return to their own country, under the conduct of *Zerubbabel*, and rebuild the temple of *Jerusalem*. But in this they were interrupted by the neighbouring nations, and the work was delayed until the time of *Darius Histaspes* (the same with *Ahasuerus*) who ordered the temple to be rebuilt, and the worship of God restored; to which undertaking the *Jews* were pressingly exhorted by the prophets *Haggai* and *Zechariah*, the former of whom prophesied that the glory of the second temple should be greater than that of the

the first; not as being a more magnificent structure, but in regard the *Messiah* should one day honour it with his presence. In the 6th year of *Darius* the temple was finished, and dedicated with great joy and abundance of sacrifices; and the Passover was also celebrated.

In the 20th year of *Artaxerxes* (445) *Nehemiah* obtained leave of the king to rebuild the walls of *Jerusalem*, in which city he likewise restored order and civil government. *Malachi*, the last of the prophets, was contemporary with *Nehemiah*, and prophesied after the rebuilding of the temple.

The *Jews* being returned into their own country, were for some time subject to the kings of *Persia*, and afterwards to the king of *Syria*. They were exposed to divers persecutions, of which the last and most cruel was that of *Antiochus*, who plundered and prophaned the temple, and made use of torments to force the *Jews* to renounce their religion, as may be seen in the history of the *Maccabees*. These cruelties obliged *Mattathias* and

H many

many other *Jews* to enter into a covenant together for the preservation of their religion and liberty. They gained many victories by the courage and conduct of *Judas Maccabæus*, and *Jonathan*, both sons of *Mattathias*: And having recovered their liberty, they reestablished the exercise of their religion, and were a long time under the government of the priests who succeeded *Judas* and *Jonathan*, and took the title of kings. At last the *Jews* fell under the dominion of the *Romans*, who made *Herod* (the son of *Antipas* or *Antipater*) king of *Judea*; and it was this *Herod* that reigned when our blessed Saviour came into the world.

Six months before Christ, *John* the Baptist was born, who was sent to prepare the way for the reception of the *Messiah*.

THE HOLY BIBLE.

PART II.

THE NEW TESTAMENT.

CHAP. I.

The Birth of CHRIST. *The* ANGEL *appears to the Shepherds. The adoration of the* MAGI. CHRIST *disputes with the Doctors in the Temple.*

THE time being at hand, when God had determined to send his only begotten son into the world, (A. M. 004) to take upon him human nature, and to dispense the gospel of salvation to lost mankind; the angel *Gabriel* was sent to a virgin named *Mary* (espoused to a man whose name was *Joseph*, of the house of *David*) whom he addressed in these words:

words: *Hail thou that art highly favoured, the Lord is with thee; blessed art thou among women.* The virgin being surprized at this salutation, the angel bid

her not be afraid; assuring her, that she, though a virgin, should conceive by the overshadowing of the Holy Ghost and bring forth a son, and call his name JESUS, who should *reign over the house of Jacob, and of whose kingdom there should be no end.* And Mary said, Behold the handmaid of the Lord, be it unto me according to thy word.

At

THE HOLY BIBLE. 117

At this time, *Augustus Cesar* having ordered a general taxation to be made throughout the *Roman* empire, *Joseph*, with *Mary* his espoused wife (then big with child) went to *Bethlehem* to be taxed: And while they were there, the time of her delivery being come, she "brought forth her first born, and wrapped him in swaddling clothes, and laid him in a manger, because there was no room for them in the inn." But though no earthly pomp attended the birth of

this

this prince of peace, yet the angel of God proclaimed the joyful news to some shepherds who were watching over their flocks by night, "and the glory of the Lord shone round about them." And when the angel had delivered his glad tidings, "Unto you is born this day, in the city of David, a Saviour, which is Christ the Lord," (whom, for a sign, he told them they should find wrapped in swaddling clothes, lying in a manger) on a sudden he was joined by a multitude of the heavenly host, praising God and saying, "Glory to God in the highest, and on earth peace, good will towards men."

The shepherds going to *Bethlehem*, and finding every thing true that the angel had said, they declared publickly what they had heard and seen, and returned praising and glorifying God. And when eight days were accomplished for the circumcising of the child (according to the law of *Moses*) he was named JESUS, which signifies a *Saviour*. He is also called EMANUEL (*Isaiah* vii. 14.
Matt.

Matt. i. 23.) which signifies *God with us*, and is the same in substance as the name *Jesus*.

When the days of the virgin's purification were over, the parents of the blessed *Jesus* brought him to *Jerusalem*, to his own temple, to present him to the Lord, and to offer such a sacrifice as the *Mosaick* law required. Thus was fulfilled that of *Malachi* iii. 1. *The Lord whom ye seek shall suddenly come to his temple*; and that of *Haggai* ii. 7. 9. *I will fill this house with glory, saith the Lord of Hosts. The glory of the latter house shall be greater than that of the former*; that is, than of *Solomon*'s temple destroyed by *Nebuchadnezzar*. To clear this prophecy it is observed, that granting the second temple, in respect to the outward ornaments *Herod* bestowed upon it, to exceed that of *Solomon* (as the *Jews* boldly affirm) it was yet inferiour to his on account of its wanting the five standing miracles or glories, viz. 1. The *Ark* in which were the two tables of the covenant; the golden pot of manna, and
Aaron's

Aaron's rod that blossomed: 2. The *Shechinah*, or divine presence, manifested by a visible cloud resting over the mercy-seat: 3. The *sacred fire* which came down from heaven, and burnt continually upon the altar: 4. The *Urim* and *Thummim*; and 5. The *spirit of prophecy*. From whence it is plain, that by the greater glory of the latter house is meant the personal presence of *Christ*, the *light of the world, the brightness of his Father's glory, and the express image of his person.*

Three learned eastern kings (called *Magi* or *Wise Men*) guided by an extraordinary star, came to *Bethlehem* and worshipped *Jesus*, bringing with them offerings of gold, frankincense, and myrrh. This star was in a threefold respect miraculous: *First*, as to place, being nearer the earth than any other star: *Secondly*, In its motion, as moving directly forwards, and not circularly: *Thirdly*, In that it shone by day as well as by night.

Soon after this, *Herod* gave the cruel orders for killing all the children in

Bethlehem

THE HOLY BIBLE. 123

Bethlehem and its neighbourhood, from two years old and under, in hopes of destroying the infant *Jesus*; but *Joseph* being warned by the angel of the Lord in a dream, fled with him and his mother into *Egypt*, where they continued until the death of *Herod*; and then, by God's appointment, they came and dwelt in *Nazareth*, a city of *Galilee*.

Now the parents of the holy *Jesus* went every year to *Jerusalem* at the feast of the Passover; and when he was but twelve years old, being with them at that

The HISTORY of

that solemnity, he tarried behind in *Jerusalem* unknown to his parents, who had gone a day's journey homewards before they missed him, not doubting but he was in the company; but having enquired after him amongst their kindred and acquaintance, and not finding him they returned to *Jerusalem* under very great concern; where, after

three days search *they found him in the temple, sitting in the midst of the Doctors, both hearing them and asking them questions;* and

and all that heard him were astonished at his understanding and answers. *Jesus* then went home to *Nazareth* with his parents, to whom he was obedient, and was brought up by them in a poor and low estate; but he *increased in wisdom and stature, and in favour with God and man.*

CHAP. II.

CHRIST, *baptized by* JOHN. *Enters upon his Ministry. His Sermon on the Mount.*

JOHN, the forerunner of our Lord, having baptized great numbers of *Jews,* the blessed *Jesus* himself (in order to *fulfil all righteousness*) condescended to be baptized by him in the river Jordan. And when he came out of the water, the heavens were opened, and he saw the spirit of God descending like a dove upon him; and a voice came from heaven, saying, This is my beloved Son, in whom I am well pleased. Here the mystery of the

most

THE HISTORY OF

moſt bleſſed and glorious TRINITY was diſplayed ; *God the Father*, by a voice from heaven ; *God the Son*, in his human nature ; and *God the Holy Ghoſt*, under the appearance of a dove.

After this, *Jeſus* was led by the ſpirit into the wilderneſs, where he faſted forty days and forty nights, and overcame all the temptations of Satan. He was now in the thirtieth year of his age, when he began to enter upon his miniſtry, preaching the goſpel of the kingdom of God, and exhorting all to repentance.

The

The truth of his doctrine he confirmed by many and stupendous miracles; the first of which was his turning water into wine at a marriage in *Cana* of *Galilee*. He went about healing the sick, curing the lame, restoring the blind to sight, casting out devils, and even raising the dead to life; thereby unquestionably proving his divine mission, that he was the promised and expected *Messiah*, who was sent into the world to make an atonement for the sins of mankind, and to purchase for all those who believed in him, and followed his most holy example, a title to eternal life.

Our blessed Lord, having gained a great number of disciples, chose twelve from amongst them, whom he named *Apostles*, viz. *Peter, Andrew, James, John, Philip, Bartholomew, Matthew, Thomas, James,* the son of *Alpheus, Simon,* called *Zelotes, Judas* the brother of *James,* and *Judas Iscariot.* These he sent forth in his name to preach the gospel, and to work miracles; and to these he more particularly addressed himself

in

in his most excellent sermon on the mount, contained in the 5th, 6th, and 7th chapters of St. *Matthew*, which may be looked upon as a summary of the *Christian* doctrine, and at which the multitude who heard him were astonished, *for he taught them as one having authority, and not as the scribes.*

The divine preacher begins his sermon with blessings on the poor in spirit; on those that mourn; on the meek; on those who hunger and thirst after righteousness

teousness; on the merciful; on the pure in heart; on the peace makers; and on those who are persecuted for righteousness sake. He tells his disciples, they are *the salt of the earth, the light of the world, a city set upon a hill*; and exhorts them, *Let your light so shine before men, that they may see your good works, and glorify your Father which is in heaven.* He commands us, if we are at variance with any one, to endeavour at a reconciliation before we make our addresses to the throne of grace. He absolutely forbids swearing, and the revenging of injuries received; and adds, *Give to him that asketh thee, and from him that would borrow of thee turn not thou away.* He teaches us, that we are not only to love our neighbour, but even our enemies; to bless them that curse us, to do good to them that hate us, and to pray for them that despitefully use and persecute us: And this from the example of our heavenly Father, who *maketh his sun to rise on the evil and the good, and sendeth rain on the just and on the unjust.*

Nor

Nor are we to imitate the Divine Being in this particular only, but in all his imitable perfections: *Be ye perfect as your Father which is in heaven is perfect.*

Our Saviour proceeds to instruct us, that we are not to give alms, nor offer up our prayers in publick places, as the hypocrites do, merely to be seen of men; but both are to be done as privately as possible, and then our Father, who sees in secret, will reward us openly. Nor are we in our prayers to use *vain repetitions, or think that we shall be heard for our much speaking:* But we are to pray after this manner. "Our Father, which art in heaven, hallowed be thy name. Thy kingdom come. Thy will be done on earth, as it is in heaven. Give us this day our daily bread. And forgive us our trespasses, as we forgive them that trespass against us. And lead us not into temptation: But deliver us from evil: For thine is the kingdom, and the power, and the glory, for ever and ever, Amen." The same rule is to be observed with respect to fasting: We are not to act the hypocrite by putting on a *sad countenance, and disfiguring our faces* that we may appear unto men to fast; but rather to avoid external shew and recommend ourselves, by sincerity of heart, to the notice of our heavenly Father. Our Lord farther advises us, to *lay up treasure in heaven*; assuring us that *where our treasure is, there will our heart be also*. And it is impossible for us to serve God and mammon, he exhorts us not to be over anxious about what we shall eat, or what we shall drink, or wherewithal we shall be clothed; for surely we cannot distrust that providence which provides for the fowls of the air, who *neither sow nor reap, nor gather into barns*; and which so clothes the lillies of the field, that *neither toil nor spin*, that *even Solomon in all his glory was not arrayed like one of these*. To this he subjoins a promise, that if we *seek first the kingdom of God and his righteousness, all these things* (i. e. food and raiment, the necessaries of life) *shall be added unto us*.

In the next place, Christ forbids us to judge rashly of one another, and condemn demns that failing to which we are all too liable, of being quick sighted and censorious with respect to the faults of others, whilst we overlook or palliate our own. He then gives this encouraging exhortation to prayer, *ask, and it shall be given you; seek and you shall find; knock and it shall be opened unto you. For what man is there of you, whom if his son ask bread, will he give him a stone? Or if he ask a fish, will he give him a serpent? If ye then, being evil, know how to give good gifts unto your children, how much more shall your father which is in heaven give good gifts to them that ask him?* To which he adds this universal and golden rule in morality, *what ye would that men should do to you, do ye even so to them, for this is the law and the prophets.* Our Lord proceeds, *enter ye in at the strait gate; for wide is the gate, and broad is the way that leadeth to destruction; strait is the gate and narrow is the way which leadeth unto life.* He cautions his followers against false prophets, who (he tells them) may be *known by their*

their fruits. And now drawing to a conclusion of his divine discourse, he exhorts them to be *doers* of the will of God, and not *hearers only*; comparing the *former* to a house built upon a rock, which is able to withstand the fury of the floods and tempests; and the *latter* to a house built upon the sand, which cannot resist the violence of a storm, but falls in the time of trial, and *great is the fall thereof.*

Chap. III.

Christ *restores the Widow's Son to Life. He stilleth the Tempest.* John *the Baptist beheaded. Five Thousand fed with five loaves and two Fishes.* Christ *walks on the Sea and St.* Peter *comes to meet him.*

WHEN our blessed Saviour had ended his sermon on the Mount he went into *Capernaum,* where he healed the Centurion's servant, on account of the extraordinary faith of his master.
And

And the next day going to *Nain* in company with many of his disciples, when he came near the gate of the city, he met a great number of people who were attending the corps of a widow's son to the place of his interment. Our Lord having compassion on the distressed woman, bid her not weep; and touch-

ing the bier he commanded the young man to arise; which he did accordingly, and *began to speak*: And he delivered him to his mother. And there came a fear on all; and they glorified God saying, that

that a great prophet was risen up amongst them; and that God had visited his people.

Not long after our saviour wrought this miracle, he went into a ship with his disciples, and as they sailed along, he fell asleep. In a short time a violent tempest arose, insomuch that the vessel

was *covered with waves*; and the disciples, apprehending themselves in the utmost danger, ran to their master and awoke him, saying, *Lord save us, we perish!* To which he replied, *Why are ye fearful, O ye of little faith!* and having rebuked

rebuked the winds and the sea, a calm immediately ensued; at which they were all astonished (as well they might) saying one to another, *what manner of man is this, that even the winds and the sea obey him?*

About this time *Herod* (the Tetrarch of *Galilee* and *Patræa*) hearing of the miracles of the blessed *Jesus*, concluded they were wrought by *John* the Baptist, whom he had beheaded, and whom he supposed to be risen from the dead. This *Herod* (we find) had married *Herodias*, his brother *Philip's* wife; and the Baptist having boldly reproved him for it as an incestuous alliance, *Herodias* resented it so highly, that she prevailed with her husband to cast him into prison and would have had him put to death; but *Herod* was afraid to proceed to that extremity, knowing that *John* was held in great esteem by the people, as a good man and a prophet. However, *Herodias* at length found an opportunity of accomplishing her wicked design; for her daughter having danced before *Herod* od on his birth day, he was so extremely pleased, that he rashly *promised with an oath to give her whatever she would ask even to the half of his kingdom.* The young woman, being before hand in-

structed by her mother, desired *Herod* to give her the Baptist's head in a charger: Upon which the king was exceedingly sorry; but for the sake of his oath, he sent an executioner, who beheaded *John* in prison, and brought his head to the damsel,

damsel, who carried the bloody present to her cruel mother.

The fame of our Saviour's miracles drew such a concourse of people about him wherever he went, that it was difficult for him to avoid their company, though ever so desirous of retirement. Of this we have an instance, when he *departed privately* with his disciples *into a desert place*; for the people being apprised of his design, he found a great multitude got thither before him, at the sight of whom *he was moved with compassion, because they were as sheep not having a shepherd: And he spake unto them of the kingdom of God, and healed them that had need of healing.* Towards the evening his disciples came to him, and put him in mind that as the day was far spent, it would be proper for him to dismiss the multitude, that they might go into the neighbouring towns and villages, and buy themselves necessary refreshments: But Jesus said, *they need not depart, give ye them to eat*; and his disciples telling him they had only five loaves and two
fishes

fishes, he ordered them to be brought; and having caused the people to sit down on the grass, he took the loaves and fishes, and *looking up to heaven he blessed and brake and gave to his disciples, and the disciples to the multitude. And they did all eat and were filled; and they took up twelve baskets full of the fragments that remained.* The number of men thus miraculously fed, were about five thousand, besides women and children.

Jesus having ordered his disciples to get into a ship, and cross over the water before him, he staid behind to dismiss the people to their respective habitations; which being done, he went up into a mountain to pray: And when he had finished his devotions, in the night time he followed his disciples, walking towards the ship on the surface of the sea. At this strange sight they were exceedingly terrified, thinking that it had been a spirit; but Jesus called to them, *be of good cheer, it is I, be not afraid.* To which Peter answered, Lord, *if it be thou,*

bid

bid me come unto thee on the water. And he said *come;* whereupon *Peter* quitted the vessel, and *walked on the water to go to Jesus;* but the wind being high, and finding himself beginning to sink he cried out, *Lord, save me;* on which our Saviour immediately stretched forth his hand to his assistance, and thus upbraided him, *O thou of little faith, wherefore didst thou doubt?* And when they were got into the ship, the wind ceased, to the astonishment of the disciples, who came and worshipped Jesus, saying, *of a truth, thou art the Son of God.*

CHAP. IV.

The good SAMARITAN. *The Prodigal Son.* DIVES *and* LAZARUS.

AS the narrow bounds of our little history will not permit us to give an account of all the miracles of our Saviour, so neither can we recite the many excellent parables he delivered

for

for the instruction of the people, but shall select a few of those that are most apt to strike upon, and affect the minds of youth, for whose use this epitome of the sacred writings is principally intended.

A lawyer asked *Jesus* this question, *Who is my neighbour?* received an answer in the following parable; which teaches us, that to *love our neighbour* is to be charitable, compassionate, ready to relieve the distressed, and universally benevolent to the whole race of mankind. "A certain man (says our Lord) went down from *Jerusalem* to *Jericho*, and fell among thieves, who stripped him of his raiment, and wounded him, and departed, leaving him half dead. And by chance there came a priest that way, and when he saw him he passed by on the other side. And likewise a *Levite* came and looked on him, and passed by on the other side. But a certain *Samaritan*, as he journied, came where he was; and when he saw him, he had compassion on him, and bound up his wounds,

wounds, pouring in oil and wine, and
set him upon his own beast, and brought
him to an inn, and took care of him.

And on the morrow, when he departed
he took out two pence and gave them to
the host, and said unto him, take care of
him, and whatsoever thou spendest more,
when I come again I will repay thee.
Which now of these three thinkest thou
was neighbour unto him that fell among
thieves; The lawyer readily answered,
He that shewed mercy on him, then said
Jesus unto him, *Go, and do thou likewise.*"

The

The parable of the *Prodigal Son* is an admirable lesson to those who have forsaken their heavenly Father, and spent their youth in vicious courses and the pursuit of vain imaginary pleasures, teaching them plainly, that no true happiness is to be found, until they return unto God by a sincere repentance, who is then willing to pardon their transgressions, and receive them again into his favour. "A certain man had two sons, the youngest of whom having received his portion, took his journey into a far country, and there wasted his substance with riotous living; and when he had spent all, there arose a famine in the land, and he began to be in want; which made him submit to the mean employment of keeping swine in the field, and he would gladly have filled his belly with the husks they fed upon. In this state he began to reflect upon his folly, and said, How many hired servants of my father's have bread enough and to spare, and I perish with hunger!

I will arise and go to my father, and say unto him, Father, I have sinned against heaven, and before thee, and am no more worthy to be called thy son; make me as one of thy hired servants. And returning home in this penitent and submissive manner, he was received by his father with open arms, who fell on his neck and kissed him, ordered him to be arrayed in the best apparel, and the

fatted calf to be killed; *for this my son (said he) was dead and is alive again; he was lost, and is found.*"

In the story of *Dives* and *Lazarus* is strongly set forth the duty of those whom Providence has blessed with riches, and the punishment that awaits them if they indulge themselves in luxury and intemperance, whilst they neglect to relieve the poor and afflicted: And at the same time the virtuous man has a comfortable assurance, that let his sufferings in this world be ever so great, he shall be rewarded with an eternity of bliss hereafter. "There was a certain rich man, (says our Saviour) who was clothed in purple and fine linen, and fared sumptuously every day. And there was a certain beggar, named *Lazarus*, who was laid at his gate full of sores, and desiring to be fed with the crumbs that fell from the rich man's table; moreover, the dogs came and licked his sores. And it came to pass that the beggar died, and was carried by the angels into *Abraham*'s bosom: The rich man also died, and was buried; and in hell he lifted up his eyes, being in torments, and seeth *Abraham* afar off, and *Lazarus* in his bosom.

And

And he cried and said, *Father Abraham, have mercy on me, and send* Lazarus *that he may dip the tip of his finger in water and cool my tongue ; for I am tormented in this flame.* To which *Abraham* answered, *Son, remember that thou in thy life time receivedst thy good things, and likewise Lazarus evil things ; but now he is comforted, and thou art tormented.*"

CHAP.

C H A P. V.

LAZARUS *raised from the Dead*. CHRIST *rides to* Jerusalem *on an Ass. The Institution of the Lord's Supper.* CHRIST *betrayed by* JUDAS, *carried before* CAIAPHAS, *and denied by* PETER.

TO the miracles of our blessed Lord already mentioned, we shall add one of the last and most remarkable that he wrought, *viz.* that of raising *Lazarus* from the dead. This *Lazarus* was the brother of *Martha* and *Mary*, whom the Scripture tells us *Jesus* loved. He had been interred four days, and was supposed to have begun to putrefy, when *Christ* came to give this signal instance of his divine power. Having ordered the stone to be removed that was laid over the grave, after a short ejaculation to Almighty God, he cried with a loud voice, *Lazarus, come forth!* And immediately the dead man came forth, though

he

he was bound hand and foot, and had his face tied about with a napkin; from

which they soon loosed him, and let him go. And many of the *Jews* who beheld this astonishing miracle believed in *Jesus*.

The time of the passover drawing nigh, *Jesus* sent two of his disciples to fetch an ass, which he had told them they would find tied at a certain place; and the ass being brought accordingly, the Lord of the Universe condescended to ride on this contemptible animal in a kind of humble triumph to *Jerusalem*, attended

attended by a multitude of people, who spread their garments in the way, and cut down branches from the trees, and strewed them in the road, crying out as they passed along, *Hosanna to the Son of David: Blessed is he that cometh in the name of the Lord; Hosanna in the highest.*

When he came to *Jerusalem*, he wept over it, and foretold its destruction; and going into the temple, he turned out the buyers and sellers, overthrew the tables of the money changers, and healed the blind and the lame.

In the evening of the first day of unleavened bread, the necessary preparations having been made, *Jesus* sat down with his twelve apostles to eat the passover. And as they were eating, *Jesus* took bread, and blessed it, and brake it, and gave it to his disciples, and said, *Take, eat; this is my body, which is given for you: This do in remembrance of me.* And he also took the cup after supper, and gave thanks, and gave it to them, saying, *Drink all ye of it; for this is my blood*

of

148 THE HISTORY OF

of the New Testament, which is shed for many for the remission of sins. At the same time Jesus gave his disciples a lesson of humility, by washing their feet and wiping them with a towel wherewith he was girded.

Our Lord, after eating this last supper with his disciples, was betrayed that very night, by *Judas*, according to his own prediction: For having retired into the garden of *Gethsemane*, to prayer (where in agony he sweat drops or clots

of blood) the traitor brought thither a
number of armed men; and saluting his
master with a kiss (which was the signal
agreed on) they seized on the blessed *Jesus* whose disciples then forsook him,
and led him to the palace of *Caiaphas*,
the high priest, where the scribes and
elders were assembled. *Peter* being will-

ing to see the event, followed afar off,
and coming to the high priest's palace,
he sat down by the fire in the hall a-
mongst the servants; one of whom,
looking earnestly at him, said, *Thou also
wast*

wast with Jesus of Nazareth. But *Peter* denied it, saying, *Woman, I know him not.* After a little while, another saw him, and said, *This is one of them:* But he denied it again. And not long afterwards, another confidently affirming the same thing, he began to curse and swear, saying, *I know not the man of whom ye speak:* And immediately the cock crew. This brought to *Peter's* remembrance the words that *Jesus* had said unto him, *Before the cock crow, thou shalt deny me thrice.* Whereupon he went out and wept bitterly.—A most remarkable instance of human frailty! For when our Lord forewarned *Peter* of this shameful fault, he promised in the strongest manner, *Though I should die with thee, yet will I not deny thee:* And so likewise said all his disciples; who nevertheless forsook him and fled in the time of trial.

CHAP.

CHAP. VI.

The Crucifixion, Resurrection and Ascension of CHRIST.

THE next morning after *Christ* was examined by *Caiaphas*, the Jews led him to *Pontius Pilate*, the Roman Governor of Judea, and accused him

of perverting the nation, of calling himself a king, and of forbidding to pay tribute to *Cæsar*. But *Pilate* finding no fault in him, did all he could to save him from

from the malice of the *Jews*; and it being a custom to release a malefactor on occasion of their great feast, he proposed to chastise him and let him go. This, however, would not satisy his inveterate enemies, who cried out loudly, *Crucify him! Crucify him!* Whereupon *Pilate*, seeing he could not prevail to save him, took water and washed his hands before the multitude, saying, *I am innocent of the blood of this just person; see ye to it.* To which the *Jews* replied with this dreadful imprecation, *His blood be on us, and our children.*

Thus wearied by their importunities and clamour, *Pilate* released *Barabbas*, a murderer, and having caused *Jesus* to be scourged, delivered him to the *Jews* to be crucified. Then the soldiers, having put a crown of thorns upon his head, mocking him, spitting on him, and offering him other indignities, they carried him to a place called *Golgotha*, where they crucified him between two common malefactors. *And there was darkness over all the land from the sixth to the ninth hour;*

THE HOLY BIBLE.   153

hour; and the veil of the temple was rent in twain, the earth did quake and the rocks rent: As if all nature suffered, when the Lord of Life and Glory expired on the cross.

One of the thieves that were crucified with the blessed *Jesus*, became a penitent on the cross, and found mercy, receiving this gracious promise from his dying Saviour. *This day shalt thou be with me in Paradise.* But we ought by no means to look upon this extraordinary case as an encouragement to a death bed repentance,

pentance, for as a great divine observes, "We read of ONE man's being pardoned at the hour of death, that none may despair, and of BUT ONE, that none may presume."

When the evening was come *Joseph* of *Arimethea*, an honourable counseller and disciple of *Jesus* went to *Pilate*, and begged his body; and having wrapped it in fine linen, he laid it in his own new sepulchre, which he had hewn out of a rock, and rolled a great stone to the mouth of the sepulchre. Now the chief priests having suggested to *Pilate*, that the disciples of *Jesus* might steal away his body in the night, and make the people believe he was risen from the dead, he granted them a party of soldiers, and *they went and made the sepulchre sure* (as they thought) *sealing the stone, and setting a watch.* But, notwithstanding all these vain precautions, on the third day after his interment, our Lord arose triumphant from the grave; at which time there was a great earthquake, and the soldiers trembled, *and became as dead men*, at the approach

THE HOLY BIBLE. 155

approach of an angel, whose *countenance*

was like lightning, and his raiment white as snow. In remembrance of our Saviour's glorious resurrection on the first day of the week, the christian church, authorized by apostolical example, keeps that day holy instead of the *Jewish* sabbath.

The blessed *Jesus*, to put his resurrection out of all doubt, shewed himself alive by many infallible proofs. He was first seen by *Mary Magdalen*, and other devout

devout women; then by *Peter* and *John*; then by the eleven; and after that by above five hundred brethren at once: And having remained on earth forty days, and spoke to his apostles *of the things pertaining to the kingdom of God*, he assembled them on Mount Olivet and there assured them, that they should in a short time receive the Holy Ghost, and *be witnesses to him both in Jerusalem, and in all Judea and in Samaria, and unto the uttermost part of the earth.* Soon after this, whilst they beheld he was taken up, and a

cloud received him out of their sight, And

as *they were looking steadfastly towards heaven* (not perhaps without some uneasiness at the loss of their dear Lord and Master) *they saw two men stand by them in white apparel,* who gave them this comfortable assurance: *The same Jesus, which is taken up from you into heaven, shall come in like manner as ye have seen him go into heaven.* Upon which they returned to Jerusalem, to wait for the accomplishment of their Lord's promise.

CHAP. VII.

The Descent of the HOLY GHOST. ANANIAS *and* SAPHIRA *struck dead for telling a Lie.* STEPHEN *stoned.*

THE Apostles, after our Lord's ascension being assembled at Jerusalem with the other disciples, chose *Matthias* by lot to take part of the ministry and apostleship, from which *Judas* had fallen by transgression; and *Matthias* was accordingly numbered with the eleven apostles. And on the day of Pentecost, to which our *Whitsuntide* answers, being the same distance from *Easter* that *Pentecost* was from the *Jewish* passover the tenth day after *Christ*'s ascension, being all met together *in one place, there suddenly came a sound from heaven, as a rushing mighty wind, and it filled all the house where they were sitting. And there appeared upon them cloven tongues, like as of fire, and it sat upon each of them. And they were all filled with the Holy Ghost,*

and began to speak with other tongues, as the spirit gave them utterance. The rumour

mour of this prodigy drew together a mixed multitude of several nations: And, to their great amazement, *every man heard* the apostles *speak in his own language the wonderful works of God.* On this memorable occasion, by the powerful preaching of St. *Peter,* about three thousand souls were added to the church of *Christ.*

By this plentiful effusion of the holy spirit, according to the divine promise, the apostles were enabled to work miracles in the name of *Jesus,* and converted many thousands to the christian faith, who constantly followed them, living all in common, and wanting nothing; for those who had estates and possessions sold them, and brought the money to the apostles, who divided it amongst the believers in proportion to their several necessities. But a certain man named *Annanias,* and his wife *Sapphira,* having sold some land, brought only part of the money to the apostles, pretending it was the whole. This being a most wicked endeavour to impose upon the Holy Ghost

Ghost by a lie, *Peter* severely rebuked *Ananias* for it, who thereupon fell down

dead at his feet, and was carried out and buried. His wife coming in soon after, and not knowing what had happened, persisted in the same story; and being also reprimanded by *Peter*, fell down and expired, and was carried to her grave by those very men who had just done the same office for her husband.—A terrible warning to all liars, hypocrites, and pretended zealots in the cause of religion!

The

THE HOLY BIBLE. 161

The number of christians increasing at Jerusalem, it was thought proper (by the advice of the apostles) to chuse seven deacons, who should distribute the alms of the whole church to the widows and poorer sort of believers. Stephen, one of the deacons, having confounded some persons that disputed with him, they falsly accused him of blasphemy, and brought him before the counsel; where the good man, *full of faith and of the holy ghost*, so boldly reprehended the obstina-

L   cy

cy of the *Jews*, and their murdering the bless'd *Jesus*, that *they were cut to the heart, and gnashed on him with their teeth. And they cast him out of the city, and stoned him, he calling upon God, and saying, Lord Jesus, receive my spirit.* Nor did the holy martyr pray for himself only, but (after the example of his great master) for his persecutors also; crying with his last breath, *Lord lay not this sin to their charge*

CHAP. VIII.

The miraculous Conversion of St. PAUL. *St.* PETER *delivered out of Prison by an Angel. St.* PAUL *shipwrecked.*

THE death of the first martyr *Stephen* was followed by a great persecution of the church at *Jerusalem*, insomuch that the believers were scattered abroad throughout the regions of Judea and *Samaria*. But among all the persecutions of the primitive christians, no one exerted himself against them with so much fury and bitterness as *Saul*, who was also called *Paul*, and became afterwards

the

THE HOLY BIBLE.   163

the great apostle of the *Gentiles*. He (as the Scripture strongly expresses it) "breathing out threatenings and slaughter against the disciples of the Lord," obtained letters from the high priest and the councils to the synagogues of *Damascus*, that he might apprehend all who professed the religion of *Jesus* in those parts and bring them bound to *Jerusalem*. But when he came near to *Damascus*, there suddenly shone round about him a light from heaven; and he fell on the

earth, and heard a voice saying to him, "*Saul*

"*Saul, Saul*, why persecutest thou me? and he said, who art thou, Lord? and the Lord said, I am JESUS whom thou persecutest: It is hard for thee to kick against the pricks." At the same time being struck with blindness, his attendants were obliged to lead him to *Damascus*, where, after three days he was restored to sight by *Annanias*, and preached the gospel in that city with great boldness, to the astonishment of those who knew the design of his coming thither, and what a bloody persecutor he had been of all that called on the name of *Jesus*.

After *Saul*'s conversion, the churches had rest throughout all *Judea, Galilee* and *Samaria*: But in a few years time, king *Herod Agrippa* observing the extraordinary progress of the gospel, raised up a persecution against the *Christians*, and killed *James* the brother of *John* with his sword. He also caused *Peter* to be apprehended, and imprisoned, intending after *Easter* to bring him forth to the *Jews*, who were pleased with his cruel proceedings. But the very night
before

before *Herod* intended to have delivered
him up to his enemies, an angel of the
Lord was sent to *Peter* in prison, who
was chained, and sleeping between two
soldiers. At the command of the angel, *Peter* arose, and the chains fell off
from his hands; and having passed two
wards, they came to the iron gate,
which opened of its own accord
at their approach; and *Peter* being now

at liberty, the angel departed. Thus it
pleased God to deliver his servant *out of
the hands of Herod,* and to frustrate the
bloody

bloody design and *expectation of the Jews*.

As to the apostle *Paul*, having escaped from *Damascus* (where the *Jews* laid wait to kill him) he came to *Jerusalem*, and *spake boldly in the name of Jesus*. From thence he went to *Tarsus*, travelled through *Syria* and *Cilicia*, and having visited divers other parts of *Asia* (chiefly in company with *Barnabas*) performing many miracles, and converting vast numbers to the christian faith, he was at last apprehended by the *Jews* at *Jerusalem*, and would have been put to death, had it not been for the chief captain of the *Romans*, who sent him under a strong guard to *Felix* the *Roman* governour of *Judea*, then residing at *Cæsarea*. *Felix*, finding the *Jews* unable to prove any thing worthy of death against him, treated him with lenity; notwithstanding which, when *Portius Festus* succeeded him in the government, being willing to shew the *Jews* a pleasure, he left *Paul* in prison.

This great apostle, as the most certain way to escape the malice of the *Jews*,
who

THE HOLY BIBLE.

who were implacably bent to destroy him, at last appealed to *Cæsar* himself; and being put on board a ship, with other prisoners, in order to be sent to *Rome* they were overtaken by a violent storm, whereby they were shipwrecked on the coast of *Melita* (now *Malta*) the vessel being beat to pieces, but every one got safe to shore. The islanders treated them with great humanity, and made a fire to warm them; but St. *Paul* having gathered a bundle of sticks, and laid

them

them on a fire, a viper came out and fastened on his hand, which made them conclude he was a wicked man, whom vengeance would not suffer to live, though he had escaped the shipwreck. However, when they saw him shake off the viper into the fire, without receiving any harm, they changed their minds, and said, *he was a God.* The apostle having continued in this island three months, curing the sick, and healing all manner of diseases, sailed from thence, and arrived safe at *Rome,* where he was a prisoner at large, and lived two whole years in his own hired house, *preaching the kingdom of God, and teaching those things which concern the Lord Jesus Christ,* without any molestation.

After this, St. *Paul* obtained his liberty, preaching the gospel in *Spain,* and then founding a church at *Crete,* constituted *Titus* the bishop of it. Then taking *Timothy* with him, he visited the churches in *Judea,* and other parts; and having ordained *Timothy* bishop of *Ephesus,* and visited the *Corinthians,* and the brethren

brethren in *Asia* and at *Troas*, he returned to *Rome*, where, meeting with Peter, they journied in preaching the Gospel both to *Jews* and *Gentiles*, until they were cast into prison, by order of *Helius*, the Governour, and offered up their lives as a testimony of the truth. St. *Paul* was beheaded, as being a *Roman* citizen; but St. *Peter* not being entitled to that privilege, was crucified.

THE CONCLUSION.

Of the LAST JUDGMENT.

AS a proper conclusion of this *History of the Bible*, we shall add a few words relating to that tremendous day, the *Day of Judgment*; a time when all mankind must appear before the judge of Heaven and Earth, and give an account of their actions in this life, whether they are good or evil. This time in holy scripture is termed, *the great and terrible*

terrible day of the Lord; the day when *the sun shall be darkened, and the moon shall not give her light, and the stars shall fall from heaven, and the sinners in Sion shall be afraid.* At this day CHRIST shall descend from heaven in his own and his Father's glory, *with a shout, with the voice of the archangel, and with the trump of God*; on which awakening summons all the inhabitants of the grave shall come forth, the living shall be changed, and all shall appear before his awful tribunal, who shall judge the world in righteousness. With him there will be no respect of persons, the monarch and the peasant will be upon a level. Small and great shall stand before him, the books shall be opened, and every man shall be judged according to his works. Then will the righteous be carried by angels of light to their seat of bliss in heaven, there to enjoy unspeakable and everlasting happiness, and the wicked shall be cast into hell, into a

place

place of woe and misery, to dwell with the devil and his angels, where *the worm dies not, and the fire is not quenched.*

FINIS.

BOOKS *for the Instruction and Amusement of Children, which will make them wise and happy, printed and sold by* THOMAS, SON *and* THOMAS, Worcester.

THE BROTHER's GIFT; or the naughty Girl reformed. Published for the Advantage of the rising Generation.

The SISTER's GIFT; or the naughty Boy reformed.

The FATHERS's GIFT; or the way to be wise and happy.

The MOTHER's GIFT; or a Present for all little children who wish to be good.

The FAIRING: Or, a golden Toy for Children of all Sizes and Denominations.

In which they may see all the Fun of the Fair, And at Home be as happy as if they were there.

Be MERRY and WISE; or the Cream of Jests and the Marrow of Maxims.

BOOKS Sold by THOMAS and Co

The SUGAR PLUMB; or sweet Amusement for Leisure Hours; Being an Entertaining an instructive Collection of Stories. Embellished with curious Cuts.

Tom Thumb's PLAY BOOK, to teach Children their Letters as soon as they can speak. Being a new and pleasant Method to allure little Ones in the first Principles of Learning.

The little PUZZLING CAP, or a small Collection of Riddles.

The big PUZZLING CAP; or a large Collection of Riddles.

The Travels of ROBINSON CRUSOE. Written by himself.

HAGAR in the Desert. Translated from the French.

The BEAUTY and the MONSTER.

The Natural History of four footed Beasts. By Tommy Trip.

BOOKS Sold by THOMAS and Co.

NURSE TRUELOVE's Christmas Box.

The ROYAL ALPHABET; or Child's best Instructor; to which is added, the History of a little Boy found under a Haycock.

The Death and Burial of COCK ROBBIN; with the tragical death of A, Apple Pye.

The remarkable History of TOM JONES, a Foundling.

TOM THUMB's Folio; or a Three penny play Thing for Little Giants. To which is added an Abstract of the Life of Mr. Thumb.

Entertaining FABLES, for General Instruction.

JACKY DANDY's Delight; or the History of Birds and Beasts.

The renowned History of GILES GINGERBREAD a little Boy who lived on Learning.

BOOKS Sold by THOMAS and Co.

The History of Master JACKEY, and Miss HARRIOT; with Maxims for the Improvement of the Mind.

The LILIPUTIAN MASQUERADE.

VIRTUE and VICE: Or, the History of CHARLES CAREFUL, and HARRY HEEDLESS, shewing the good Effects of coninued Prudence.

NURSE TRUELOVE's New Year's Gift, &c.

New SONG BOOK.

A little LOTTERY BOOK for Children: Containing a new Method of playing them into a Knowledge of Letters and Figures, &c.

www.ingramcontent.com/pod-product-compliance
Lightning Source LLC
Chambersburg PA
CBHW022113160426
43197CB00009B/998